Confidence & Joy: Success Strategies for Kids with Learning Differences

A Step-by-Step Guidebook for Parents and Professionals

Dr. Deborah Ross-Swain, Ed.D., CCC-SLP
&
Dr. Elaine Fogel Schneider, Ph.D., CCC-SLP, BC-DMT, CTTIT

Crescendo
PUBLISHING

Confidence & Joy: Success Strategies for Kids with Learning Differences: A Step-by-Step Guidebook for Parents and Professionals By Dr. Deborah Ross-Swain, Ed.D., CCC-SLP & Dr. Elaine Fogel Schneider, Ph.D., CCC-SLP, BC-DMT, CTTIT

Crescendo Publishing, LLC
2-558 Upper Gage Ave., Ste. 246
Hamilton, ON L8V 4J6
Canada

GetPublished@CrescendoPublishing.com
1-877-575-8814

ISBN: 978-1-948719-12-4 (p)
ISBN: 978-1-948719-13-1 (e)

Printed in the United States of America
Cover design by SAM ARTS

10 9 8 7 6 5 4 3 2 1

Message from the Authors

This book is a result of more than 70 years of combined clinical work with children and their families who experience communication disorders and learning differences. Our clinical work represents professional experience that collaborates with parents and professionals to create opportunities for learning success that can build confidence and joy in children struggling with learning differences. Collaborating with other professionals and providing families with educational and service resources can result in children reaching their potential.

All children are different, and all children want to succeed. You have in your hands a powerful book that can make a huge difference in the lives of children with learning differences, their families, and the professionals and educators who serve them.

You will learn why confidence and joy are important, how creating meaningful relationships can build confidence and joy, and what can be confidence and joy robbers.

You will discover the signs and signals of learning differences, how to jump-start your child's confidence and joy, and how to go to bat for your child.

Moving from isolation to teams and communities of support, you will recognize how all children are smart in their own way. You will be inspired by anecdotal stories about children with learning differences and how they and their families turned their lives around.

By using the valuable tools provided in this book, you will be inspired to provide opportunities for increased awareness, growth, and achievement to secure each child's personal, educational, and social success—in addition to your own.

Gifts from the Authors

We are happy you have chosen to read our book. To help you implement the many different points presented in each chapter, we have prepared the following bonus gifts especially for you:

A downloadable, easy-to-read list of *Points To Consider*™ for parents and professionals to keep close at hand, each day:

10 Confidence & Joy Points to Consider™ to Maximize Each Child with Learning Differences Potential for Success

A fact sheet of scientific studies that supports the importance of bringing confidence and joy into the lives of every child with differences:

Science Supports Success for Children with Differences

Get instant access to these complimentary materials here:

http://theswaincenter.com or http://askdrelaine.com

Endorsements

"Wise, practical guidance for parents and educators of all children, especially those who learn differently from extremely experienced and compassionate professionals. This book is about building confidence and joy in children, especially those with learning differences. Moving, touching on-target stories are included that lead to deeper understanding and effective interventions. The reflections sections provide guidance for parents in growing their effectiveness and skills. They serve as excellent discussion prompts for parents and professionals. This book is an excellent resource and tool for parents and educators."

— Robert L. Hendren, D.O.
Professor of Psychiatry
University of California, San Francisco Department of Psychiatry & Langley Porter Psychiatric Institute
University of California, San Francisco Weill Institute for Neurosciences

"I highly recommend this book to parents, teachers, and care providers for children with learning differences or special needs. There are many books out there about how to diagnose and try to fix problems, but this one, Confidence and Joy: Success Strategies for Kids with Learning Differences, focuses on the crucial issue of creating and maintaining confidence and joy in every child, which are the deepest keys to success."

— Sanford C. Newmark MD
Director Pediatric Integrative Neurodevelopmental Program
Osher Center for Integrative Medicine
University of California, San Francisco

"Confidence and Joy: Success Strategies for Kids with Learning Differences provides inspiration and guidance to parents and professionals who are involved with children with learning differences who often have educational, social, and emotional challenges to face. Drs. Swain and Schneider compassionately describe the progressive decline in these children's self-esteem over time and the various "robbers" of joy and confidence which lead to the decline. They discuss recommendations on how to manage them. The authors emphasize that it takes community and school support as well as active parental advocacy to preserve and promote the confidence and joy children are born with and that it is these feelings which lead to emotional well-being, success, and the ability to tackle obstacles in the course of their lives."

— Cathryn Ross, MD
Developmental Pediatrician

"Confidence and Joy: Success Strategies for Kids with Learning Differences is for all parents, care-takers, and educators who care for and educate children who learn and develop in atypical ways. Drs. Swain and Schneider are clear about what is important for all humans, and especially for children who feel different - positive and meaningful relationships, experiencing and feeling confident. They remind us that intervention is important but feeling connected and good about oneself is essential for a fulfilling life."

— Dan Peters Ph.D.
Psychologist
Cofounder/Executive Director, The Summit Center
Author: From Worrier to Warrior; Make Your Worrier a
Warrior; Raising Creative Kids

"Dr. Deborah Ross-Swain and Dr. Elaine Fogel Schneider once again have described eloquently the problems that many children face when they try to contend with difficulties in learning. Their wise counsel and years of experience as clinicians have shaped their thinking into the need to provide such youngsters with good feelings about themselves so that they can feel confidence and joy. We often overlook that need and think that if we, as clinicians, provide services such will correct other aspects of their lives and well-being. Well, wait until you read their chapters where they describe such youngsters, their giftedness, and their need and treatment for building confidence and joy in this world."

— Donna Geffner, Ph.D., CCC-SLP/A
Past President, American Speech-Language-Hearing Association
American Speech-Language-Hearing Association Honors
Donna Geffner and Associates

"Drs. Ross-Swain and Fogel Schneider's timely and groundbreaking book provides guidance and hope for parents with children with learning differences. It also provides insights for professionals, and shows how every child with learning differences can find confidence and joy, and be successful. Children with learning differences are often robbed of their confidence and joy, and parents often feel isolated. The valuable strategies provided in Confidence and Joy: Success Strategies for Kids with Learning Differences can be readily integrated into daily routines, and serve as tools for change. The feelings of "I don't belong" and "I can't do anything" can be transformed into "I belong" and "I can do this!" This book is a gem, and one that needs to be read and shared by parents, professionals, and students."

— Joel Stark, Ph. D., CCC-SLP
Professor and Director Emeritus
Speech-Language-Hearing Center
Queens College, City University of New York

"The authors of this book "get it"! They understand the challenges of children and their parents who are struggling in school. By adding the keys of confidence and joy, lives are changed and learning begins. I was one of those children who did not learn to read. I really did try harder! My parents and other adults were supportive. I was creative and good at art which I believe saved me. I learned by listening, thinking and watching until I finally caught on. I started out slow but became very successful. I am on my 4th CEO job. I am a happy and successful adult. Help children discover how they learn and use that to move them into other subject areas. Learning differences are better than learning difficulties. But children still don't like to feel or be different. We can stress each child's unique interests and abilities to show that we are all different."

— Kay M. Marquet
Chief Executive Officer
Canine Companions for Independence

"There is an alternative to the child's too common transition from innocent joy to alienation. The erosion of confidence and joy for children with learning differences is tragically overlooked in our education system. Drs. Swain and Schneider's new book delivers recognition and a path forward that is essential for parents and educators to learn and undertake if we are going to guide our children in the most meaningful endeavor of becoming and sharing what can be gained through appropriate education."

— Lina Foltz
Special Education Attorney

"The connection between happiness and our health is the secret sauce to doing well in school and in life! Dr. Deb Swain and Dr. Elaine Fogel Schneider provide an easy and insightful read on how confidence and joy contribute to a child's success. Deb and Elaine are angels and among the best educational and healthcare professionals and resources you could ever find to help your child, you, your families, and your communities. Confidence and Joy: Success Strategies for Kids with Learning Differences is a small treasure in an ocean of how much it can positively impact children's lives."

— Donna Downs Kawasaki, MBA, EMBA
Innovative Global Solutions

"Confidence and Joy: Success Strategies for Kids with Learning Differences is an important book for parents, professionals, and University students. Drs. Ross-Swain and Fogel Schneider combine their experiences and knowledge to bring home the importance of developing confidence and inspiring joy for children with learning differences. Thoughtful, easy-to-use strategies and checklists make the content interactive for the student or the parent and a useful tool for the educator. This is a "must have" book for libraries with an academic audience and/or libraries for the general public."

— Kristine Holloway; MLIS, M.Ed.
Associate Librarian
California State University, Bakersfield

"This is an important resource for family members and professionals working with children with learning differences. It can be very easy to get caught up in clinical and academic interventions and forget the often negative feelings that can sideline a student who is struggling. Confidence and Joy: Success Strategies for Kids with Learning Differences is a great reminder to step back and remember that we want our students to also be happy and enjoy their learning experiences and feel good about themselves!"

— Stacy Frauwirth, MS, OTR/L

"As a mother of twins with learning differences, I know from experience their daily struggles, as well as my own. Drs. Ross-Swain and Fogel Schneider have brought together a common sense and inspiring book, with practical strategies that are definite calls to action for parents everywhere. These strategies can be easily used to discover and bring out the confidence and joy that lie within every child with learning differences. As a parent, by reading this book, Confidence and Joy: Success Strategies for Kids with Learning Differences, I am strengthened, feel more hopeful and see ways to uncover the confidence and joy within my own children, so they can thrive and succeed. I wish every parent, educator, and/or professional who works with children with learning differences reads this book. Our kids deserve to live confidently and joyfully. This book leads the way!"

— Jackie Billera, CLC
Parent of Twins with Learning Differences
Certified Life Coach at Bee My Life Coach

"This powerful book should be read by every parent, grandparent, and professional who has a child or works with a child with a learning difference. Drs. Ross-Swain and Fogel Schneider are miracle workers. They have shown me so much and my granddaughter is the better for it. I am so pleased to see how my granddaughter tackles problems with a confidence she did not have before. She continues to develop her talents and perseveres with a joyful attitude. I am so proud of her success. What else could a grandparent hope for?"

— Grandmother of RH
Palmdale, CA

Table of Contents

Dedication

Tens of thousands of children, adolescents, and adults have struggled with learning differences during their school years. They have also struggled with self-confidence, self-esteem, and the ability to achieve and maintain a sense of sustained joy and happiness. These individuals have served as our teachers and heroes as they worked tirelessly to achieve success. This book is dedicated to each and every one of them and their families, who also strive for their child's confidence, joy, and success!

Introducing:
Confidence and Joy

Confidence and joy are to the development of a child as oxygen is to life! Every child deserves to experience confidence and joy in order to grow, achieve, and prosper. It is the responsibility of parents and professionals to get our children from little people to big people with confidence and joy in their hearts. It's as simple as that!

We, the authors, are speech-language pathologists and have more than 70 years of combined experience working with children with communication disorders and learning differences. We have observed, firsthand, the daily struggles and challenges faced by children with learning differences and the toll such differences take on their spirit, emotional health, and overall well-being. We make the distinction between learning differences and learning disabilities. These children are NOT disabled. They are quite capable of learning everything their peers learn. They just learn in a different way.

Most of the children we have had the pleasure of working with have average and above average intelligence. Some have superior intelligence. These kids are not in special education per se, but may have an IEP for reading or math support or no IEP at all. These are kids who do not have a diagnosis or label such as Learning Disability. These are smart kids who are misunderstood and often frustrated by their learning differences. They are misunderstood because of their brightness. They "look" smart, and therefore should be able to learn and achieve like their peers. When this doesn't happen, words such as "lazy," "inattentive," "unfocused," "oppositional," or other such words are assigned. These are smart kids who have a different learning style. The sad truth is that when children have a different learning style, they typically feel they are "dumb" or "stupid" when in fact they are not. Their individual learning style does not allow them to succeed with traditional teaching methods. They just learn differently and should not be penalized for having differences.

Over the years of working with these amazing kids, we know that their learning differences don't let them learn the same way their peers do. Not only do we know this, but they also know it and so do their parents. Unfortunately, they struggle with reading, spelling, or math day in and day out. They struggle with their sensory system, not knowing how to pull apart a sealed luncheon wrapper or zip up a zipper, or button a button. They may not be able to focus on the teacher or classroom lesson of the day. They may not know the words to use to enter into a conversation with classmates, or how to make friends. Yet they have to go to school each day and do the same thing they did the day before, and the day before, and the day before. This pattern only makes them feel worse and worse about themselves. It is little wonder that school-aged anxiety, depression, and isolation appear to be on the rise.

As adults, we have privileges children don't have. By law, they have to attend school. If we adults had to do something every day that made us feel bad about ourselves, we wouldn't do it! We would instead find something that would foster success so we could experience confidence and happiness. Children with learning differences struggle far too much—and their struggles, circumstances, and daily encounters often rob them of confidence and joy. They don't get to experience success though they try their very best. They don't enjoy learning as they once did as preschoolers. They typically don't like school because of the way they feel when they are in school. We have to change things so learning differences are not viewed as negative, but rather as opportunities for discovering and revealing a child's gifts and talents. We have to give every child the opportunity to experience success in a learning environment. Success builds confidence, and confidence brings happiness or joy. Confidence and joy are game changers for children and provide the foundation for growing emotionally healthy little people.

All children want to learn and be successful. Preschoolers are a perfect example. They love to go to school each day and find wonder and joy in just about everything they do. Because preschoolers are still developing and meeting milestones, learning differences are not as visible. Learning differences typically aren't realized until children enter school—when reading, spelling, and math are introduced. Then, the once learning inspired and successful child meets head-on with failure. They work hard and try their very best to "get it," but they can't. They have a learning difference. So, despite their very best efforts as well as their persistence, they can't succeed. As goes success so goes confidence and joy.

The next ten chapters are dedicated to ways in which parents and/or professionals can build confidence and joy in children with learning differences. This book has significant information on what learning differences are and what they are not; why confidence and joy are necessary and important; the value of relationships with others in building confidence and joy in children; the signs and signals that what you are seeing as a behavior problem is really a reflection of a child's frustration with a learning difference; strategies for "jump-starting" your child's confidence and joy; how to go to bat and advocate for your child with learning differences; the value of building a child's confidence and joy team; creating communities of confidence and joy; and understanding that every child wants to succeed and ways to make it happen.

Finally, we have participated in thousands of IEPs or other similar team meetings. So much of the discussion is around the goals and objectives for improving reading, spelling, and math in order to assist children in being academically successful. It is our hope and vision that in the future, similar goals and objectives will be included in formal documents specifying measurable strategies designed to improve and sustain a child's confidence and joy. These will help raise happy and successful children, who will then become happy and successful adults.

1

So, Your Child is *Different*

Jacob is a second grader who struggles to learn. Learning hasn't been easy for Jacob since he entered kindergarten. Jacob loved to learn, explore, and try new things when he was in preschool, but that changed when he started school as a kindergartner. He appears to be just like his peers, except that he has a really difficult time learning to read, spell, and understand math. Despite his best efforts and the efforts of his parents, Jacob still struggles. Jacob is bright, very talented in sports, and liked by all his peers. Jacob realizes he needs lots of extra help that his friends don't need, and that he goes to a "special teacher" to help him learn. But learning isn't getting easier, and now Jacob feels different. He is saying to his parents, "I'm different"; "I want to be like the other kids"; "I don't like school"; and "I can't do anything right." Worst of all, Jacob has let "different" become his identity. Jacob is unhappy at school and has no confidence, embarrassed that he can't be more like his friends.

What Does Different Mean?

It seems as if educators, parents, and our culture have allowed "different" to be wrong rather than what it is. Different means not the same. It is as simple as that! Yet Jacob represents so many children who are bright, talented, and gifted, but are feeling bad about themselves because so much weight is put on the negative perception of being "different."

The universal truth is that *all* children are different. The problem is that we place so much value and weight on what others perceive as *normal* without really understanding that all children are not only different, but special. Why is different and special a problem? Mostly because parents, teachers, and society in general have an expectation of what "normal" is and what "different" isn't. In most cases, different means *special*— and not necessarily in a good way. This is particularly true when it comes to school, academics, and social relationships.

Let's begin by looking at the concept of *different*. What makes a child different? A child can have learning, communication, relationship, physical, sensory, or social differences. But children can also be different because of their gifts, such as art, movement, dance, music, subject matter expertise, sports, technology, creativity, acting, singing, and working with animals. Children can have learning differences *and* be talented in sports, music, art, etc. So, why are differences in an academic sense magnified without consideration of a child's gifts? Unfortunately, in our culture, success is measured by academic achievement and not so much by the "gifts" that a child possesses.

Now, what about the idea of different versus special? We all want our children to be happy and successful. When a child has learning differences, they often feel that they are not successful. Not just academically, but with everything. This is especially true for children with undiagnosed learning difficulties, who struggle to learn or keep up with their peers— who they perceive to be successful with schoolwork and on the playground. Unfortunately, there are many, many children who struggle with reading, spelling, math, and overall learning, as well as social interactions. Yet most are not eligible for special education services or school-sponsored tutoring programs. These children are often misunderstood, as they appear to "not try," "not listen," "not get along well with others," or "have a bad attitude." Maybe there are times when their peers begin to perceive these children as "not smart," when in fact they *are* smart—but how to best access the child's abilities has not been identified yet. What is actually very important for parents, educators, and other professionals to keep in mind is that not all children learn the same. That is, all children have their own learning style, even though many *look* as if they all learn the same.

What About Learning Styles?

The term "learning style" can be interpreted differently, depending on who you are asking or the context. Generally, most will refer to learning styles as visual, auditory, or kinesthetic (touching and/or movement). But research indicates that learning goes beyond just visual, auditory, or kinesthetic learners. A child may be an auditory-visual learner. Another child may be an auditory-kinesthetic learner; yet another may be a visual-kinesthetic learner. Finally, a child may be a combination of all three learning styles. But learning is also influenced by a child's emotional system, as well as his/her psychological state on any given day. It is up to parents and teachers to discover a child's learning style as well as watch and note learning response behaviors that can reveal lots of information as to how a child can be a successful learner.

For example, a parent or teacher may note that a child has a slower processing speed that can make the child look like they are not understanding information or remembering what has been said—and possibly "not listening" because they just can't keep up. Another behavior may be that a child has difficulty transitioning from one topic to another, but can do so successfully when the adult says, "Now, we are doing something different." Another behavior is the child who is most successful when instructions are given one-to-one rather than in a group. Giving this child instructions one-to-one can be very time consuming, but is essential to building his/her academic success. Recognizing this one little change in a child's learning style and ability can make all the difference in the world for the child, but it can be tricky for a busy classroom teacher tending to a large number of students!

Finally, there is the child who is the multisensory learner. That is, the child who needs information presented in all three ways: auditory, visual, and kinesthetic. It becomes necessary for parents and teachers to become "learning-style" detectives to learn a child's most effective and efficient learning style in order to find the best way for a child to learn and be successful. When a child's learning style is identified, learning can then take place. Is it a magic bullet? Of course not! Will it make learning easier? Yes. Will a child still have learning differences? Yes, of course. Is this okay? Yes!

The important thing is that learning styles be recognized, and problems associated with learning differences are minimized and success is maximized. Otherwise, learning differences interfere with a child's success, and they begin to feel different and unsuccessful. Kids are smart. They realize that other children are "getting" what they are not; they are working on a task that they themselves don't understand, understanding what the coach is saying, or getting classwork done efficiently. So, despite working hard, paying attention, listening, and doing their homework, school isn't getting any easier. As a result, they feel less and less successful and more and more different! This is not a good combination for building confidence and joy in a child.

The Universal Parenting Tip

We tell our children from a very early age, "If you keep trying, it will get easier." This parenting tip begins as young as the toddler learning to walk. We tell the preschooler who is learning to ride a scooter or bicycle, "Keep practicing and you'll get it." For the future piano protégé, we say, "The more you practice, the better you will be." Unfortunately, we often say the same thing when a child is struggling with reading, spelling, writing, math, and overall learning. But when a child has learning differences, the old adage "practice makes perfect" doesn't work. What does work is finding out what a child's best learning style and environment is, and getting it in place so success can happen.

Parents, teachers, tutors, and other professionals have to agree to stop telling the learning-different child that "practice makes perfect" when it just doesn't! Doing the same thing over and over again with no change or improvement is just wrong. This practice, unfortunately, is all too common and does nothing for a child except make them feel worse and worse. This book is about building confidence and joy in children. So, anything a child is doing that doesn't result in improvement, achievement, and successful outcomes has to be stopped. Finding way(s) to make the child successful must be started. The adults in the lives of children have to realize that when "practice makes perfect" isn't working, then it's time to figure out what to do to make it work! There absolutely are ways to get a child learning, and sometimes we have to "think outside the box." The onus is on us, the adults in the lives of children, to make it happen!

All Children Want to Be Successful

Yes, it's true. All children want to be successful! Early childhood is full of successes: rolling over, crawling, walking, throwing a ball, and putting a puzzle together are just a few examples. Picture the preschool years and the delight on the face of a four-year-old attending preschool. Learning is exciting, fun, and structured in a way that makes a child feel successful. Preschool programs and teachers are experts in introducing new skills and activities in a way that ensures fun, delight, and achievement. These little ones can't wait to come home and tell or show their parents what they learned in school. These settings are necessary for helping children learn and master skills and concepts they will use when they are enrolled in kindergarten or a transitional kindergarten. These little ones are learning in ways that are fun and engaging. They love to learn because of how the learning makes them feel: happy, confident, secure, and accepted.

The nice thing about preschool is that there is more "wiggle room" with learning, because there is so much developmental difference in those early years. So, though preschoolers reach developmental markers at different times, they still feel success and are happy learners! Not only are they happy learners—they are filled with confidence and joy. They are unaware that they may have learning differences. They embrace learning with eagerness, enthusiasm, happiness, and confidence because the learning environment feels good and staff is committed to children's achievement and success. These little ones learn early on what success feels like and how it makes them feel. Yes, all children want to be successful!

The 'Learning Different' Child After Preschool

For children with learning differences, traditional learning may change for the once happy and successful preschool learner. Most public educational systems have core standards that children must meet. Children with learning differences can have difficulty meeting core standards because of their learning style. Their learning style may not work with the teaching style of the classroom teacher. Or, the child's learning style may not work with the way a particular reading program is taught. It is our job as parents and educators to make a child feel successful even though learning differences challenge a child's achievement and success. Keeping in mind the happy preschooler who loved learning, we want to keep that joy of learning alive for the elementary school child as well.

Once a child enters school, there are two types of success: academic success and social success. When children are academically successful they "look" like the other kids; they perform like the other kids and have similar outcomes. When children are socially successful, they have lots of friends, are accepted, are invited to birthday parties and playdates, and are included in other social activities. When children struggle academically or socially, they feel unsuccessful. But more importantly, they tend to lose their confidence and their self-esteem suffers.

Do their differences make them wrong? Do their differences make them weird? Do their differences make them unacceptable? Do their differences make them unworthy? Absolutely not! Their learning differences make them who they are. That's it. They are just like all the other children, but need someone to help them "figure it out" in order to learn and achieve. It is up to the adults in their lives to assist them in achieving success and recognizing that differences don't make them bad or wrong, but make them the person they are; they are special, unique, wonderful, bright, and full of potential. Every child is special, and we need to celebrate who they are, all that they are, their unique contributions, and their own successes. If children perceive that their only road to success is measured by classroom achievement and they can't meet the expectations, then parents begin to regularly hear, "I can't do it"; "I'm stupid"; "No one likes me"; "My teacher doesn't like me"; "I'm the only one who can't do this"; or "I never get picked for a team." This negative self-talk must be avoided at all costs! It doesn't have to happen if differences are minimized but not ignored, and talents and gifts are highlighted, as well as learning styles identified and instruction adjusted to match the learning style. If all of this is done consistently so as to become a habit, then the adults in the child's life will have done their jobs.

Children Know

Children are amazing human beings. They learn by watching and listening. They can put two-and-two together really fast—even before some adults. This can be a blessing and a curse, especially when they have learning challenges. Children know when they are struggling more than their peers. They know, because they can't do what the others in the classroom are doing. They know the other kids aren't getting one-on-one help. They know the others aren't taken to the back table for help. They know the others don't have to stay in at recess to get work finished. They know that others can read words on a page and they can't. This is where the adults come in to "rescue" the struggling child from becoming unhappy and anxious about school, losing confidence, and eroding self-esteem. This needs to happen early. Waiting is not an option, because too much is at risk! Parents and teachers must form a "team" to figure out a way to make learning feel good and a child feel successful. Nothing is more important!

Parents of Kids Who Are Different

It can be really tough for parents to accept that their child may have a learning challenge or social differences that will interfere with their success and perceived potential. Parents need to recognize it—and be okay with it—to help make learning feel good and success happen. Some parents may go into a denial mode and want to give the child more time to mature or practice their reading and math. Other parents may ignore the problems and assume he/she will "outgrow" the problem. Others may blame the teacher for "poor teaching." Other possible reactions can be guilt, shame, or anger. None of these reactions are useful or productive.

What is useful and most productive is an open and ongoing conversation with the child's teacher, resource specialist if applicable, and other school personnel. Knowing exactly the nature and extent of the learning difference then empowers parents to be responsive rather than reactive. Responsive parents are moved into action to assist the teacher in identifying a child's learning style, making learning successful, building the child's confidence, and highlighting a child's gifts. The adult team is key to creating success for the child, as well as keeping healthy self-esteem and confidence. Sometimes, the learning "baby steps" need their own baby steps to break down a lesson enough to achieve success.

It Really Does Take a 'Village'

Parents can't do it on their own, and neither can teachers! The "village" is created intentionally by proactive parents and teachers. Typically, this can be started with a Student Study Team (SST) or Individualized Education Plan (IEP) when a child is enrolled in public school. When a child begins struggling in school, it's best to consult teachers or other educational professionals to determine if the struggle is "typical" for a child's age or goes beyond what is considered "typical." Taking a "wait-and-see" posture or allowing time to "outgrow" the difficulty is not a good idea at all. The longer a child struggles with learning and continues to be "behind" his peers, the greater the likelihood that secondary problems can arise. Like Jacob, there is potential for the learning differences to become a child's identity accompanied by negative self-talk, poor self-esteem, and a lack of confidence. So, gathering the SST or IEP team can change a child's course when learning differences are identified.

When parents and educators work together for a child's individual success, *different* doesn't have to be negative. More importantly, the language used around the learning different child has to be different. That is, everyone has to stop saying things like: "You need to listen better"; "You need to try harder"; "Pay attention"; "Don't worry, you'll get it"; "When I was little I had the same problem"; "Everyone struggles"; or "Stay in at recess to get your work done." None of these are true, and none of these will make learning fun or easier. The child with learning differences needs the work to be broken down into manageable and successful baby steps so learning can take place and they can *hear* and *believe* affirmations such as: "You did it"; "You are so bright"; "You can do so many things that others can't do"; "You are so creative and a great problem-solver"; "You are a leader"; "It was hard, but you did it so well"; and other positive, affirming, and confidence-building statements. They have to hear these statements consistently and from many sources to really believe they are true. It can be helpful to teach a child self-affirming statements that they can say to themselves daily. Some affirmations can include: "I am smart"; "I am important"; "I am good at _____"; "I am a good listener"; and others you may think of. The child's *village* should have an open discussion and plan about the language of learning and success for the child, and commit to putting it into action. The road to confidence and joy begins with creating and inspiring success in children. For the learning different child, this is as intentional as teaching reading, spelling, and math.

Reflections

1. What makes my child different? What are my child's strengths?
What are my child's weaknesses?

2. How does my child learn best?

3. What can be done to make my child feel happy and successful
with learning and being with friends?

4. What does my child's village look like?

5. What do I need to do to make my child feel happy and confident about learning?

2

Why Are Confidence and Joy Important?

Jonah wakes up each morning and goes to bed each night singing. He is always humming and enjoying the music of life, although his body may not function as smoothly as other children his age. He runs with his wrists and hands flailing outwards to try to keep his torso strong. He attempts to hop on one foot at age five, only to fall down after one hop. He is still joyful, although not fully confident in his skills. He worries about his own success, comparing himself to others his own age and even younger. He sees that his younger brother can do things that he cannot, like put his shoes on the right foot, pull up his own socks, and put on his own clothes. All his clothes... underwear, pants, shirt, socks, and shoes. When it comes to talking and speaking clearly, Jonah has difficulty. He doesn't use plurals, and mispronounces some sounds. He is a loving and beautiful boy, who sometimes has his emotions get the best of him as he lashes out and points his finger at his mother or father.

Jonah is also the kid who sits at the table and cannot sit still. He puts his fingers in his mouth, his ears, his nose—and then he may smell his fingers when that is all done. He is the one who doesn't mind his hair all over his eyes, the one who does not know how to keep a conversation going between other children. We may rehearse in our own mind "until we get it right" before going to a party or a dance. Jonah wants to get it all right on the first attempt at anything he does. But it takes him an attempt and then another attempt and another to "get it right." Then, he has to learn it all over again the next day, because his motor planning is poor. His body needs the consistency of doing things over and over and over until his body senses what he needs and can deliver. For Jonah, life is joyful, though. Although he lacks confidence in his skills, when comparing himself to others, he continues to improve and make daily strides. He's proud to show you his new accomplishments, like being able to peel off the backing of a sticker and open up a water bottle. He is becoming more successful each day, and is experiencing greater confidence and joy in that success.

How Do You Define Confidence?

Confident children are children who know who they are and can take risks. Confident children feel good about themselves and are willing to raise a hand in class to ask a question and/or answer a teacher's question. The confident child is willing to learn new things, even when the answers are not clear. The confident child can explore and learn and grow, because he knows that whatever he learns will be more than what he knew before. There is no judgment voiced in his own head. Other people's judgments do not concern him, either.

Being confident is being present to discover for discovery's sake. No fear, no shame, no guilt... Learning is just that—*learning*. Confidence is like putting one foot in front of the other to walk, then picking up one foot to skip, and then increasing your speed so you can run, and then running with abandonment. Confidence is knowing that you have whatever it takes to accomplish a task.

Confident children are sure of themselves. They know they can achieve if they "get into the game." Confident children may have self-talk going on inside themselves that is positive. They may say, "I am strong!"; "I can do anything!"; "I can move mountains." Confident children are resilient. If at first they can't succeed, they keep trying again until they do.

Confidence is the antidote to anxiety in children. When a child knows he will not succeed at reading a passage, or writing a story, or climbing across the monkey bars like his classmates, he becomes anxious. He may not even want to try. Confidence can propel a child to attempt a math problem. Confidence can prompt a child to say "hello" to a fellow classmate and engage in play activities with peers. Confidence can encourage a child to pick up a basketball for the first time and play in front of unknown spectators, without shedding tears of failure. Confidence is knowing your own mind, knowing your own emotions, and knowing you can achieve—even if you are different from other children.

Being confident in yourself is a vital tool for success. Being confident and joyful allows you to face each day with the knowledge that no matter what comes your way, your attitude—not just your aptitude—makes you successful.

How Do We Measure Joy?

Joy! What a wonderful word! We all savor those moments, events, activities, and people that bring us joy! The importance of joy in our lives is not new information. As a matter of fact, we are told by historians, scientists, authors, and philosophers around the world that joy is essential for our well-being and lies deep within our hearts and bodies. Waking up with joy each day is like a hidden treasure. You feel the ecstasy of greeting each new day and wondering what it will bring. Like a sunrise, each one is different; yet each one is glorious.

We all have the opportunity to wake up and greet each day with a joyful and happy heart, right? Sure, but as adults, we are often distracted by "stuff" like work, bills, family, and other commitments.

But what about children? Joy and happiness is their business! Children find joy and happiness in just about everything they do. They laugh, squeal with delight, and giggle as their eyes light up with just waking up and greeting the world each day. Every day brings so many opportunities for children to experience joy— eating their favorite foods, watching their favorite cartoons or shows, playing with their favorite games and toys, learning new things, playing with their special friends, singing, dancing, running, and so much more. But what happens to the joy of children who have trouble learning, dressing, eating, making friends, running, skipping, riding bikes, and keeping up with their peers? What happens to their parents' joy?

Parents report how their hearts are broken when they see their children struggle day after day. For children with motor planning difficulties, getting dressed can be a chore. Not knowing how to put their arm through a sleeve, or how to pull a sock over the heel of their foot, can be exasperating. For children who have a feeding difficulty, having a chunk of peach left in their peach yogurt can send them "over the top." Many despair when they can't reach a bell to ring at the top of a rock wall. Others, when playing Monopoly, may lack the joy of deciphering a card that reads, "Get out of Jail." There are millions of children who face each sunrise with little joy, as do their parents.

What do you do when there is no joy? As adults, you know there will be challenges you will face, with life's ups and downs. You know what brings you joy, and you can pick and choose. Children do not yet know about themselves that way. They may know that things are hard for them. They may notice they cannot do things their siblings or friends can do. As an adult, you have the wherewithal to know things have a way of working out. Like a little child, you can find the gold within the treasure box of life.

To Feel Joy, or Not Feel Joy

For children with learning differences, life can be filled with sadness and despair. Joy does not come easily to them. Yet some children may be born feeling confident, believing they are strong and can do anything—even lift mountains. Some may feel confident, and others weak. Some are ready to face the day and value their worthiness. Others dread the idea of getting dressed to go to a place where challenges, rather than solutions, arise day after day.

Waking each day with joy in your heart means that even though there are struggles or challenges, you can still experience happiness. Joy for being alive. Joy for eating your favorite ice cream flavor. Joy for being surrounded by people who love you. Being joyful means you are looking at the glass half full and not half empty. Through the darkest hours of despair and being different, there are moments of joyfulness too. With an attitude of joy, you can get through the day feeling blessed to be alive. When you are in your darkest hours, it is that joy in your heart that radiates to others, that brings others into your circle and attracts others to you. An attitude of joy will keep you going.

The Dalai Lama and Archbishop Desmond Tutu refer to lasting joy as a way of living with "shining contentment." Born from deep well-being, joy is nothing less than exploring what makes the human experience satisfying.

Joy can bring a smile to your face, a dance to your step, and a swagger to your walk. You've seen when a child has a walk of confidence and a sense of belonging. Confidence builds a person. Confidence is empowerment and a springboard for hope. Synergy comes from confidence and joy, and a zest for life for all that comes your way—and all *who* come your way, too.

You Are Your Child's First Teacher

Children look up to their parents as their first teachers. They also look up to their teachers. So, it is important that parents and teachers demonstrate their own confidence and joy so a child can mirror those characteristics growing up and experience how it feels to be joyful.

As a parent or teacher, you may question your own level of joyfulness and confidence. It is important that you are present to your own emotions, since you are your child's first teachers. They look to you for guidance, support, and love. You may be inconsistent in the way you live your own life, which can affect your child's behavior and emotions.

Here are some questions to ask yourself:

- Do you get depressed when things don't go your way?
- Do you become upset or angry and raise your voice when your children are not doing what you think they should?
- Are you condescending in the way you speak to your child, who is learning new things (i.e., learning how to put on a shirt, how to ride a bike, or how to use the "potty")?
- Do you lose your own joy when you find yourself showing your child with a learning difference the same thing over and over again?
- Do you catch your child doing something wrong more often than catching him doing something right?

5 Easy Ways to Encourage Confidence, Joy, and Success

For a child who is different, his sense of self-worth may be low. He may compare himself to others. His anxiety may hold him back from participating in games, contributing to class discussions, or making friends. As parents and teachers, what can you do to promote feelings of well-being, confidence, and joy?

1. *Encourage learning by using the way your child processes information best.* Each child's DNA (nature) makes up who he is, including temperament and learning style. The family he was born into and the environment in which he lives nurture your child. Both nature and nurture have important roles in your child's learning. Understanding them and optimizing them will lead to your child's success.

2. *Create learning experiences that include your child's interests.* Children do best when they are interested in a topic. When you see your child gravitate toward an object, book, or place, see what it is and expand on that topic. If your child likes candy and has a speech delay, for example, label the candies and increase speech sound production. If your child loves the park and has movement concerns, figure out which equipment would be best for body movements, strengthening, balance, etc., and be a "kid again" yourself.

3. *Refrain from comparing your learning different child to a sibling, cousin, or any other child.* For example, have you ever heard a parent say (with good intentions): "Why can't you sit up straight like your sister?" Well, if he could sit up, he would. He is a different learner. His core muscle strength is weak. He sits up better when a pillow is put behind his back. He sits better on a large ball. Instead of intimidating your child, realize your child is a different learner and encourage his better posture without comparison.

4. *Praise your child's strengths and do not "call out" his weaknesses.* All children, even those who are different learners, have strengths. Praise your child's kind heart, or sweet smile. Praise your child's ability to share with others, or his sincerity in asking how you feel when he sees you are upset.

5. *Have fun with your child!* Making learning tedious with a "to do" list can bring everybody down. Give your child your undivided attention for just five minutes a day. No siblings allowed. Let him be a leader, and you the follower. Let him

do what he wants, within reason (i.e., play ball his way, go on a scavenger hunt, or just cuddle on the couch). He is in control now, and there is no right or wrong way of doing anything.

Success brings confidence and joy. Children (and adults) become more confident and joyful when they are successful. By knowing which ways your child learns best, making topics of interest available, not comparing him to others, praising his strengths, and letting him be a leader for five minutes a day, you can bring out the best in him. From this success, innate confidence and joy grows.

Trash Trucks to the Rescue

Devona was a five-year-old who held a pencil without using a pincer grip (three-finger hold), and preferred using her hands to eat at mealtimes. Knowing she loved trash trucks, and learned information bodily-kinesthetically and verbal-linguistically, her teacher introduced several fun activities. A golf tee was introduced to Devona, which she called a "drill." The object of the activity was to use a pincer grip to hold the golf tee and "drill" a hole in a paper towel (a regular sheet of paper was too difficult at first, so a softer paper towel was introduced). Then, by using the golf tee more, she moved it through the hole to make the hole larger. She laughed and giggled, determined to poke more and more holes through the paper towel. When the hole was even larger, she used her index finger to poke through the hole and enlarge it even more. Then, using her thumb and index finger, she ripped the paper into little pieces. She put the paper into toy trash bins she had lined up ready for trash collection. Her toy trash trucks picked up and hauled off the trash to the recycling yard. This fun activity added to Devona's confidence and joy.

Her whole body engaged in the activity. She felt the golf tee in-between her fingers as she pushed the "drill" through the paper. Then, she poked her finger into the hole. As she ripped the paper, she further engaged her bodily-kinesthetic learning. Using words like "drilling" "piercing," "poking," "tearing," "putting in," "hauling away," etc. engaged her verbal-linguistic style of learning, too!

In just a few weeks, Devona's new learning transferred to her skills at the dining room table. When having dinner with her family, she confidently and joyfully picked up a serving spoon and began stirring the mac and cheese that was in a bowl near her. Holding the spoon correctly, she scooped it out without dropping any off the spoon. She put a serving on her plate. For the first time, she independently and successfully served herself, proceeding to "stab" the mac and cheese with her fork!

The "drill" activity presented to her made learning fun and allowed her to excel, without squashing her passion for learning and exploration. Poking and ripping with a unique object kept her interest, and transferred over to her new skills (stirring, scooping, and serving)—to the surprise and delight of her parents.

Differences, Not Disabilities

For the child who is a different learner, "confidence and joy do not come easily" is an understatement. Legs may not hop. Bottoms may not be able to lift off the floor while doing a yoga bridge. Crossing the monkey bars is a struggle. Listening to a teacher reading a book can be painful. Memorizing spelling words is futile. Speaking clearly so others understand may not be an option. Holding a pencil and writing neatly may be challenging. The learning different child is different, and he knows it. Yet these differences need not be viewed as disabilities. Parents and teachers need to embrace these differences to discover the ways their child learns best. Mr. Rogers asserted those who have lost hope, who live in disappointment and bitterness and find no joy or love in life, are the real disabilities. Everyone is different—even identical twins! Confidence is a springboard for hope and builds a sense of empowerment and joy within. *Success brings confidence and joy. Confidence and joy bring success.* Confidence, joy, and success are synergistic and interrelated. When a child has confidence and joy, it's not that they can't do it. It's a resounding, "I can do it, and just did! Hooray for me! Hooray for us!"

Reflections

1. What kind of attitude does your child generally demonstrate each day?

2. When does your child seem to show confidence in his skills? Is there a pattern?

3. When does your child demonstrate joy? Is there a pattern?

4. What is your child's natural learning style that will springboard his way to success?

5. What is one special thing your child would like to do? Create a learning experience around it.

3

Relationships: Shape You, Make You, and Celebrate You

Lily is a pretty fourth grader who has struggled in school since Kindergarten. However, early on, her preschool teachers noticed not only some learning delays at that time but also some social delays. As a preschooler, Lily had difficulty learning her colors and alphabet letter names, recognizing numbers, and creating relationships with her preschool friends. When Lily struggled in class she would whine, cry, and have tantrums, making the other students uncomfortable and standoffish. At recess, if Lily didn't "get her way," she would act out in the same way. Soon, other children didn't want to play with her. As time went on, she wouldn't be invited to birthday parties or playdates.

Lily was diagnosed with dyslexia and ADHD in the second grade. She was pulled out of class for special tutoring and academic support for part of school day. Lily could often be impulsive in her behavior, as well as awkward with her interactions with others. Because of her struggles, Lily has many weekly appointments for tutoring, therapy, and counseling, leaving little free time to participate in socially-oriented activities like dance, soccer, or gymnastics. Lily desperately wanted to have friends, but really wasn't sure how to make and keep friends, so she has become withdrawn and spends large amounts of time with her family pets and solitary activities such as drawing, beading, and using her iPad.

Lily's parents are very concerned, because when they participate in activities with other families, Lily is withdrawn and tends to go off alone. She tells her parents, "I am dumb"; "Nobody likes me"; "The kids at school make fun of me"; and "I hate school." Lily cries before school every day and is often late to class because she refuses to get out of the car when they get to school. Lily's parents have tried family counseling, tutoring, and structured playdates. They are so worried and concerned, and are even considering homeschooling. They feel that Lily has no confidence and her sadness and desire to withdraw are because she does not have friends at school. Her parents are committed to finding a way to help her make and keep friends now, so she will feel valued and liked by her peers.

Relationships Matter

Kids love being with other kids! *Being in relationships* starts really early in a child's life. When children are part of a toddler play group, relationships begin and children love it. As a matter of fact, *everyone* enjoys and benefits from being in a relationship with others—from being liked and accepted. Most of us seek out meaningful relationships throughout our lives. Secure and happy relationships bring everyone a sense of belonging and comfort. Actually, our relationships may be one of the most important pieces of our lives. They are really important in the lives of our children, particularly when learning differences may have already affected their confidence in making and keeping friends—or being *liked* by others.

All children want to be liked and accepted by others, whether the *others* are children or adults. The first relationships that we have are with our parents. Parents and their newborn children enjoy the most loving and passionate relationships ever. It is through these early relationships that babies first experience the joy, happiness, adoration, comfort, and security that happen only through intimate interaction with other humans. From very early on, children *get* the importance of positive relationships.

After the initial parent-child relationship, other relationships begin to happen. They expand to family, extended family, and family friends. Ultimately, our children will be in relationships with many people in a relatively short period of time. So, other than family and friends who our children are in relationships with, who will be influencing them?

Relationships for Kids

Believe it or not, any other person who our children have consistent or ongoing interactions with will be the people they have relationships with. These individuals can be nannies, sitters, daycare providers, teachers (preschool, Sunday school, classroom), tutors, coaches, counselors, physicians, dentists, neighbors, school peers, scout or club leaders, and many more. To build happy, joyful, and confident children, the relationships our children have with others must be happy, healthy, respectful, and secure. For some children, this is an easy process. For others, not so much.

Children with learning differences can also have difficulty making and keeping friends. For school-aged children, there are two types of success: academic success and social success. Learning differences already implies that academic success can be a problem. But the thought of social success being a problem is often overlooked. Kids naturally make and keep friends, right? Not really. Depending on what is causing the learning difference, many of these kids find it difficult to form fun and stable friendships. They have difficulty *understanding and learning* the "social rules." These kids can't comfortably or effectively navigate the social network that looks so simple, but isn't. They may have trouble with appropriately greeting others. They may not be aware of social boundaries or turn-taking and flexibility. Some may have no filter and blurt out things that are not socially appropriate or acceptable. Then, there are kids who are inappropriately affectionate or clingy. Some are too silly, cry too easily, have meltdowns, or are easily irritated. Social navigation can be really difficult.

Why Can Social Relationships Be Difficult?

Many of us know kids who can be socially odd or "quirky." These are kids whose behavior or communication is "unusual," "peculiar," or "different." Often, they have trouble "fitting in" with their peer group. They say and do things that make others uncomfortable or annoyed. When this happens, some kids and adults find it hard to like and appreciate their quirkiness—which then makes it difficult to be in relationships with others. Why is that? What is the problem with kids who are different? There are no simple answers to these questions. But it's clear that being rejected or feeling like "nobody likes me" can be really hard on a child. It is also hard for parents to watch this happening to their child. When building relationships isn't automatic or natural, social skills have to be taught—just like reading, spelling, or math. There are many children who want to have social relationships with their peers but can't because of their "quirkiness" or differences. When this happens, confidence and joy can erode.

Parenting the Child with Social Differences: 5 Strategies for 'Figuring it Out'

As parents, we all want our children to have friends. Often, their struggles become our struggles. Parenting a child who is struggling with relationships can be challenging and emotionally exhausting, because parents experience so many different emotions when their children struggle. Parents can feel sad, anxious, defensive, guilty, frustrated, or even angry. Parents feel bad when they are told by teachers or other adults that "Your child doesn't get along well with others"; "Your child says inappropriate things"; "Your child doesn't listen to instruction"; "Your child doesn't follow rules"; "Your child is mean to other children"; "Your child won't share"; or "Your child cries and pouts too much." These are things that can interfere with a child's ability to make and keep friends or have healthy, fun, and stable peer and adult relationships. So, what's a parent to do?

Because having stable and healthy relationships is so important to the well-being of a child, as well as necessary for building a child's confidence and joy, parents need to be very strategic and intentional in planning and implementing a process for assisting their child in building relationships. Basically, keep in mind that some children have to be *taught* how to "do relationships." Here are a few helpful strategies to get you started in helping your child:

1. Take an inventory of your child's social skills. You may need the assistance of a professional with this, such as a speech-language pathologist, behavioral therapist, or psychologist.

2. Determine what behaviors are getting in the way of your child's ability to make and keep friends.

3. Have a heart-to-heart, open, and honest conversation with your child's teacher. Find out what his/her perspective is and what they observe in the classroom and on the playground.

4. Observe your child in a variety of social situations. Try to be like the proverbial "fly-on-the-wall" so your presence doesn't change the dynamics of the situation. You may want to look through the window of the classroom, watch your child on the playground at recess, watch an athletic practice, observe and listen to what happens between your child and

another during a playdate, or watch your child engage with other children at a park play area.

Once you have figured out what the problem behaviors are, you are ready to help your child make meaningful relationships with others. Your role here is to be a "social detective" so you can ultimately help your child develop meaningful relationships with others to build their confidence and joy.

Looking Closely at Your Child's Relationships

Because relationships are so important to *all* children, and are fundamental to building confidence and joy, it is necessary that everyone involved in children's lives be committed to making sure that healthy, stable, and happy relationships are a priority. These types of relationships would include those with both children and adults. Determine who the key people are in your child's life. Ask these questions:

- What is the status of these relationships?
- Are these healthy, nurturing, stable, and happy relationships for your child?
- Are they building your child up?
- Do you see your child becoming happier and more confident because of these relationships?
- Are they mutually beneficial?
- Do you see struggles or unhappiness?

These are all important questions to be asked and answered, particularly when there is a problem with relationships.

One of your child's most important relationships will be with his/her teachers each year as they journey through their school years. Teachers have a tough job managing and teaching a classroom of students with different needs. However, these same teachers have a significant amount of influence on your child's confidence and happiness. When your child is having difficulty with academic success, request the support of the teacher. Let the teacher know that your child is struggling with confidence, is unhappy, or doesn't like school. Find out what the teacher can and is willing to do to assist in making your child feel and appear to be successful in classroom activities that are not related to academic success. What can the teacher do to make your child feel liked, valued, and appreciated? How can the teacher facilitate building sound and happy relationships between your child and the other students? Maintaining consistent and frequent contact with the teacher can ensure that you both are working on a shared goal: building your child's social successes, confidence, and joy through developing happy and meaningful peer relationships.

Making Time for Friends

Children with learning differences tend to be involved in many outside activities that are intended to make their life or learning easier. They may be going to regularly scheduled tutoring sessions or other similar programs. They may be going to speech or occupational therapy or counseling. When parents select a tutor or therapist, it must be done with a careful "eye". You need to know how to scope out the best person for your child. Though a tutor or therapist may come highly recommended by a friend or neighbor, that person may not be a "good fit" for your child. Once the tutoring or therapy process begins, that marks the beginning of your child's relationship with that person. Will this person build your child's confidence, joy, and happiness— not only academically, but socially? Will this person make your child feel respected, appreciated, and accepted?

Tutors and therapists are so important in a child's life, because they have the skills and experience to help a child achieve success in academic areas where they have been struggling. As many parents who have been working with tutors and therapists over a period of time know, the amount and rate of therapy progress can vary. This is where a skilled and wise tutor or therapist is important. The type of relationship established between the child and tutor or therapist has the potential to create a safe and secure *friendship* while building skills necessary for achieving success. The tutor and therapist should understand the value of their role so as to challenge the child without judging or allowing feelings of failure or defeat. These professionals become the adult friend who, through skilled instruction, can build your child's success *and* confidence. What a gift! Most parents are really good at reminding their children how much they love them, how bright they are, how talented they are, and how great they are. But let's face it: you are the parents, and kids assume it's your job to say those things. When kids are struggling in school or with relationships, they kind of don't believe you. They need to hear it from others they value and respect. So, a tutor or therapist can be that kind of person if they're the right person for your child.

Relationships Build Up a Child

Never underestimate the power of healthy and meaningful relationships. Building these relationships should be as important as ensuring your child's academic success or selecting the school your child will attend. Why? Every child needs to be liked, accepted, respected, and valued for the person they are. Sure, there are times when kids can be mean to each other, and say and do hurtful things. But they still have friends. When your child is having difficulty making and keeping friends, then you must step in and help make it happen. Parents can begin by modeling healthy and meaningful relationships with their own friends. They can model respectful and mutually beneficial relationships with people in their community who are not necessarily close, intimate friends. They can put down their electronic devices and model face-to-face communication and interaction. They can take time to not only have friends, but be friends. Parents of children who struggle with social relationships often have to advocate for their children when it comes to making and keeping friends.

5 Strategies for Helping Your Child Make and Keep Friends

As mentioned earlier, parents can—with the help and input from others—be "social detectives." After you have gathered the necessary information, you can get to work creating opportunities for your child to begin the process of making and keeping friends and building happy, fun, healthy, and secure relationships. Here are a few suggestions:

1. *Be proactive* when it comes to relationships for your child. Don't wait for your child to "get it." If you notice that your child is struggling socially or doesn't have a close circle of friends, it is important to act earlier rather than later. Make a list of all opportunities your child has on a weekly basis, and use those to engage and interact with others. For example, if your child attends a church and participates in a children's program, talk to the teachers and give them guidance for engaging your child so he/she does not get isolated or engage inappropriately. Connect with other parents whose children are participating in the same program and arrange for get-togethers. Or, if your child has after-school daycare, talk with the director about your concerns and see how he/she can help. Relationships where a child feels liked, accepted, secure, and happy will build his/her confidence and joy.

2. *Enroll your child* in activities such as Boy Scouts, Girl Scouts, 4-H, or other social clubs for children. Talk to the leader about your child's specific social needs and the need for relationship-building. These types of activities are great for building lasting and healthy relationships, as well as making your child feel liked and accepted by his/her peers.

3. *Ask your child* who he/she really likes in their class or outside activity. Contact the child's parents and express that your child would like to have a playdate. When the child does

come to your home, have a start time and end time. Select activities that are interactive and ones you can facilitate if need be. This takes time and energy, but arranging *regularly* scheduled social activities for your child will allow him/her to build skills for developing healthy, happy, and supportive relationships. Your child will feel liked and accepted, and you will see changes in his/her confidence and joy.

4. *Enroll your child* in a sport or music and arts program. Be sure to let the coach or instructor know that your child has difficulty with some skills or has learning challenges so they can provide individual instruction whenever possible. Also, if your child has attention or listening difficulties, the adult leader won't think that your child is being difficult or inattentive. You can give them specific strategies to make this a successful activity for your child. These types of activities provide an opportunity not only to develop other skills, but also to develop relationships. Both of these will then build confidence and joy for your child.

5. *Get involved* in community programs or activities as a family. There are other families just like yours who want to make a difference in the lives of others, but also in their own child's life. When you select a community program or project, make sure your child is engaged with age-level peers as well as other adults. Be sure that your child has a specific task that he/she can be praised for completing. Get together with other families with children so your child can engage and interact socially and frequently. These interactions can result in short- or long-term relationships, and both are important. They have the same potential outcome: being liked and appreciated, which builds a child's confidence and joy.

Final Thoughts on Relationships

Parents are urged to be sure their children are involved in relationships that are sound, healthy, happy, meaningful, and respectful. Everyone wants to be liked and accepted by others. This is a basic human need. Adults are very aware of the importance of being liked, accepted, and valued by others. "Others" can include friends, co-workers, employers, and neighbors, as well as strangers. When we consistently don't feel liked and accepted, we are not happy and don't feel confident. The same is true for our children. For children, the stakes are higher, because they haven't had the life experiences of adults. As adults, we have a greater ability to navigate the social network. We have greater social opportunities and can create opportunities to be in relationships with others. Our relationship-building opportunities go beyond school and home. Being in sound, healthy, happy, and stable relationships is a fundamental human need. It has to happen for our children in order to build confidence and joy. Confident and happy children grow into productive, happy, and secure adults who can then face the challenges that will come. Relationships shape us, make us, and celebrate us!

Reflections

1. What are my child's strengths and weaknesses with relationships?

2. What situations are most difficult for my child when it comes to relationships?

3. Who are the people that my child has sound, secure, and stable relationships with?

4. What are the specific action steps I will take to assist my child in feeling liked and accepted by others?

5. What did I learn about my child when I became a "social detective"?

4

Confidence and Joy Robbers

Adam is a bright fourth grader who has struggled socially in school since Kindergarten. He was diagnosed with ADHD in the middle of the first grade. At that time, his teacher was concerned with his inattention, hyperactivity, lack of focus, and verbal and behavioral outbursts. She reported that he was impulsive when interacting with other students and "had no filter." Her biggest concern was that Adam could not make and keep friends. He could not understand social "rules," and was often perceived as being inappropriate or "too physical." He was not invited for playdates or to birthday parties because his friends were a bit scared of him. He often spent recess time in his classroom, getting schoolwork completed because he couldn't complete it during class. Over time, Adam became unhappy and didn't want to go to school. His parents moved him to a different school in the second grade and another in the third grade. Adam really struggled with social skills, and one day, he pulled a chair out from under a classmate as a joke. As a consequence, Adam's dad had to come to school and sit with Adam for the remainder of the school week. Adam was embarrassed and ashamed. Again, he felt different and isolated. Unfortunately, these situations and circumstances have robbed Adam of confidence and joy.

The Loss of Confidence and Joy

There is nothing that makes us feel worse than having something taken from us. It can be something material, a dream, a plan, or a feeling. When something is taken from us without our permission, we can react with anger, frustration, sadness, or dismay. When something tangible is taken away from us without our permission we can call authorities, report it to insurance, or simply replace it—right? But what about feelings, emotions, or thoughts? What do we do when those are taken from us, when they are robbed from us? What happens? Well, most of us will react with feelings of sadness or maybe hopelessness and helplessness. As adults, we hopefully have developed adequate coping skills to deal with this type of loss. We can learn from other similar experiences, change our environment, work with a counselor, talk with family and friends, or figure out how to reconcile the loss and move on. We typically *know* we can move forward and still be happy and confident as adults.

Confidence and Joy Loss in Kids is a Big Deal

What about kids? What happens when their confidence and joy is taken from them—not just occasionally, but consistently? It's our job as parents and adults to get our children from little people to big people with confidence and joy in their hearts. Confident and happy children can grow up to be happy, secure, and confident adults. But some children more than others are at risk for not experiencing confidence and joy consistently—enough that the absence of these feelings becomes their *way of being.* Children with learning differences are typically in situations where learning isn't easy or successful, and they "aren't getting it" or seemingly can't do what their peers can do despite their very best efforts, massive amounts of tutoring, extra classroom help, and accommodations. They feel unsuccessful and may say things like "I'm stupid"; "I'm not smart"; "I never get things"; or "I can't do it." These kinds of thoughts and feelings can and do make kids feel sad, frustrated, different, ashamed, and lacking in confidence.

This chapter is about confidence and joy robbers: situations, people, events, or activities that, knowingly or unknowingly, *rob* children of confidence and joy. Most people don't even think about this happening because children tend to be happy, joyful, and confident—right? Not really. Those robbers can happen subtly, such as a small incident, comment, reaction, or look. Most children don't even know that it's happening. Kids just know that they don't feel happy and confident in certain situations or around certain people. Parents notice that their once happy child has gradually become a sad and unhappy child who is lacking in confidence and has low self-esteem.

Most parents will move heaven and earth to create opportunities or situations that will make their child happy, and they do... temporarily. A movie, a trip to the ice cream store, a new toy, or a special playdate are fantastic ways to make children happy. But when kids are in situations or activities where they can't feel successful fairly consistently, those things that parents do to make them happy are only temporary remedies to a chronic problem. When kids experience constant unhappy and defeating situations, they become victims of *confidence and joy robbers.*

The Risk of Confidence and Joy Robbers

Typically, most people are unaware that they are placing a child in a situation or activity that may rob them of confidence and joy. Just one situation or a few random situations are not going to rob a child of these important gifts. It's when it happens daily, when it's a pattern—when a child is constantly struggling or isn't experiencing success. That's when a child is at risk for being robbed of confidence and joy.

The Overuse of Clichés

Adults use lots of clichés with children. Some seemingly innocent expressions are: "You need to try harder"; "Your brother can do it, so you should be able to do it too"; "You need to spend more time practicing"; "How many times do I have to tell you?"; "I've told you a hundred times"; or "You did it yesterday, why can't you do it now?" For the child with learning differences, who has trouble remembering things when he/she hears these expressions too often and with a tone of frustration, these comments can have a negative impact. It doesn't matter if the comments are heard from a parent, teacher, or other important person; the effect will still be the same. The overuse of clichés and expressions such as these are confidence and joy robbers.

More Vitamin S

A lack of success can be a huge confidence and joy robber. Every child has to experience success. Success is highly empowering. Success begets success, and is a powerful catalyst to building confidence and happiness. Children with learning differences have a tough time being successful, especially when it comes to academic subjects like reading, spelling, and math. Some may have difficulty being successful in social situations too. In the minds of children, there are two types of success: academic and social. When a child feels unsuccessful in these areas and parents are finding their child feeling frustrated, unhappy, tentative, lacking in confidence, or withdrawing, they have to act fast to find *something* their child *can* be good at. This should be something that enables them to shine, builds their confidence, creates success, and allows their peers to see their area of talent.

When your child is struggling with reading, spelling, and math, get them involved in a sport, hobby, or some activity where they can stand out and really shine. If they don't like or have trouble with team sports, try individual sports. If they aren't interested in sports, then try music, art, crafts, dance, acting, construction activities, or working with animals. Just be careful here not to go from one activity to another, trying to find the best activity, because that may make your child think they can't master something. Parents need to be strategic about identifying what would be "a good fit" for their child. Take time to observe your child and see not only what they can be good at mastering, but also what they enjoy doing. Put these two pieces of information together and you can create the perfect activity that makes your child feel successful. The feelings of success will build confidence and joy in your child.

Homework Hassles

For the child who struggles in school, homework is the worst! For parents of children with learning differences, *homework hassles* after a long day are just plain frustrating and painful. When children struggle to learn, homework is a reminder of what they *can't* do. Children spend approximately six hours a day in school learning new information. Then, they are assigned homework to practice this new learning. That's fine for the child who doesn't struggle. Let's face it: most children don't love homework, but they can get it done independently and in the expected time frame. But for the child who struggles, they frequently don't want to sit down to do the homework. They can't do it independently, so they need a parent to sit with them and move them through the assignment. Then, they find it takes way longer than it should, and crying, pouting, and/or tantrums start. The reason for this is that they struggled during the day and now are struggling again at home. They felt bad about themselves during school hours, and now they get to feel bad about themselves again. Homework hassles and all that goes with them is another confidence and joy robber.

Yes, children need to practice new skills with their academics, but parents should work with teachers to create the best homework plan for their child to help the child feel successful, meet homework expectations, and practice new learning—

while at the same time building mastery of skills (modifying homework and taking baby steps). Consistent success then makes a child feel like they are progressing. This combination creates confidence and happiness. Parents and teachers can work together to contain this confidence and joy robber.

Is it Feedback or Criticism?

It's our job to give our kids input. Sometimes, even our best intentions can be perceived as criticism. Criticism is another confidence and joy robber. Criticism *feels* negative and hurtful, whereas feedback and input *feel* more positive and less hurtful or critical. We know that adults don't intend to sound critical, but often say things that can *feel* critical—especially when they are said too often and not balanced with positive compliments.

You may be thinking that children need feedback or *constructive criticism* in order for them to excel. Yes, input is important for every child—but *what* is said and *how* it is said are just as important. Kids are smart, and they know the intent behind what is being said. They are also aware of how often they hear it.

Criticism doesn't motivate children; it robs them of joy. It robs them of confidence. It's not unusual for children who are struggling to hear comments like "You never listen"; "You always forget your assignments"; "You can't get along with your friends"; "You aren't organized"; or "You are always too slow." These comments do nothing to improve the situation or outcome, but when heard often, they will make a child feel bad or even defeated. Changing comments so they sound more positive and supportive can make a huge difference in how a child feels. Try saying:

- "I need you to listen," rather than "You never listen."
- "Oh, you forgot your assignment—let's email your teacher and get a plan for helping you remember your assignments," rather than "You always forget your assignments."

- "I like how you are trying," rather than "You need to try harder."
- "I know you can do it," rather than "Why can't you do it?"

Don't let what you say and how you say it rob your child of confidence and joy.

Tutoring, Tutoring, Tutoring

Excessive and intensive tutoring or therapies can be confidence and joy robbers, especially when children have been doing these things for several years. When children are struggling in school, they may receive special assistance from school-sponsored programs, or parents may seek out tutors for reading, spelling, or math as well as speech, occupational, or behavioral therapies. Actually, this is the right thing to do. But when these services go on for long periods of time, are producing minimal changes, and look like they will never come to an end, children can get discouraged. They feel like they will never be able to master anything without outside help. This can be a confidence and joy robber!

Along this line, if a child moves from one clinician to another for the same type of therapy and progress is still a bit slow and stagnant, the child begins to feel like there's really something wrong with him/her. Kids get burned out on remedial programs and therapies when they are never-ending and aren't helping. These ongoing and intensive programs not only rob them of confidence and joy, but also of time. With all the therapies and tutoring, there just isn't enough time to "be a kid" and hang out with friends, participate in sports or recreational activities, or get involved with other social things. So, parents need to be careful and wise in selecting programs intended to make their child more successful.

The Dreaded B Word: Bullying

Unfortunately, children with learning differences can be targets for bullying for no other reason than the fact they're different. Bullying in any form is incredibly hurtful and a huge robber. When children are ridiculed and bullied, the message to them is, "You are different or weird and we don't like you," or "You are not like us; you aren't accepted." Younger kids who don't have a lot of social experience don't understand the reasons behind bullying. They just know that their "friends" don't accept them and they don't know why. This erodes confidence and self-esteem. It takes away their joy. Older children understand the social fabric a bit better and know that through bullying and ridicule, they are being excluded and targeted as different. It doesn't matter the age—bullying and ridicule from peers will cause significant unhappiness and, potentially, isolation. Bullying, big or small, robs children of their confidence and joy.

Consequences: Yes or No?

Another confidence and joy robber is something that is fairly common and not typically seen as harmful. But when it happens with other confidence and joy robbers, it can have a huge impact. This one is *consequences*. Children with learning differences often take longer to get their assignments completed on time. They may have attention problems, making it difficult to listen. They may be easily distracted or have difficulty focusing for long periods of time. The problem with these behaviors is it may look like a child is *intentionally* working slowly, not listening, not focusing, or being distracted. Depending on the underlying cause, these kids just can't work faster, listen, attend, or focus. Because a child looks like they *can* but *doesn't*, they get in trouble in the classroom or with coaches or other leaders. They get **consequences.** Some common consequences may be:

1. Having to stay in at recess to complete their work because they work too slowly

2. Having to do work during an art project because they couldn't focus during the lesson

3. Having to sit outside the classroom because they talk too much

4. Having to miss a class party because they were distracted and were distracting others

5. Being assigned extra homework because they didn't get their work completed in class

6. Spending lunch time in the administrator's office to get classwork finished, because they consistently aren't getting their work done during class time

These consequences are meant to motivate a child to work faster, listen more, focus better, and get assignments done efficiently. The problem is, they typically don't work. If the underlying problem is with how a child's brain is working, there are no amount of consequences or punishments that will change them. These types of consequences are really punishments. A child is being punished for the way his/her brain works. If they could change it, they would. What consequences do is make a child feel even more different and isolated. Consequences for the learning different child are a punishment for behaviors that a child has no way of changing without the help of skilled professionals. Consequences, when imposed frequently and over time, are a huge confidence and joy robber.

Being Alone is Never Good

Isolation can be a confidence and joy robber. Children who struggle can often feel and become isolated. Their struggles in school and socially can make them withdraw from interacting with others. These are children who may prefer to play alone, with younger children, in the company of adults, or with electronic devices. The lack of human interaction and joy that engaging with friends brings can be a confidence and joy robber. Choosing to withdraw or be isolated because of prior rejections, ridicule or bullying, or feeling uncomfortable can interfere with social growth and maturity. But it also allows a child to have some control over their environments and situations so they don't have to feel bad. The use of electronics for games and entertainment has become popular, but they are not a substitute for engagement with others. Being a wiz with electronics is a great skill and can be one of the things that makes a child stand out among peers if it's not intended to isolate them. Otherwise, however, electronics are not empowering. They don't build confidence, and rarely result in lasting happiness. Mastery and competency derived from excellence with electronics will not prepare a child for adulthood. What may appear to be confidence builders now aren't long term. Children, all children, are social creatures and are intended to engage and be involved with other children. Isolation may be a reaction to problems associated with learning differences, but should not be a way of life. Isolation can make a child feel lonely, unhappy, and have low self-esteem. Don't let isolation rob your child of confidence and joy that human interaction and engagement can bring!

There are other confidence and joy robbers you can list. It's important for parents to be on the lookout for any person, activity, or situation that is a confidence and joy robber and eliminate it. Remember, it is the responsibility of parents and professionals to get children from little people to big people with confidence and joy in their hearts.

Reflections

1. What are the confidence and joy robbers in my child's life?

2. What brings my child confidence and joy?

3. What are new activities I can do to build my child's confidence and joy?

4. What am I doing to rob my child of confidence and joy?

5. What are others doing to rob my child of confidence and joy?

5

Signs and Signals:
See, Feel, and Act

Alex is a beautiful eight-year-old boy who absolutely hates school and all the kids in his classroom—but especially he hates his teacher, Ms. Moody. When you meet Alex, you notice his sensitive eyes, halting speech, and inability to sit still. You see him looking around the room and fidgeting as he moves from one side of his chair to another. He then stands up and sits down, trying to get himself comfortable. He is given a writing assignment in class, only to find that his classmates can go to recess because they completed their work, but he must stay inside and work on the writing project until it is finished. His teacher tells him, "You've had plenty of time to finish this writing assignment, just like the rest of your classmates, but they finished it and you just can't seem to finish anything you start. So, you can stay in the room until you get it done!" If that wasn't bad enough to destroy Alex's confidence and joy, who is doing the best he can, Ms. Moody shouts this out for the entire class to hear. In Ms. Moody's eyes, Alex is a failure.

In Alex's eyes, he is a failure—and now the rest of the class knows it, too!

Warning Signs – What are Red Flags?

What were the signs Ms. Moody missed? She missed that Alex was not purposefully leaving his work incomplete. Kids *want to do well*. She missed that by keeping Alex inside, he didn't get the exercise his body needed to get his "fidgets" out. Alex also lost the opportunity of socializing on the playground. Moreover, his other classmates will pick up on the teacher's negativity. Any chance of Alex having friends who would empathize with him or support him became impossible, as his classmates picked up on Ms. Moody's negativity.

For parents, red flags are the signs that pop up—some subtler than others—to make you **stop** and **wonder** what is going on with your child. There are some distinctions that need to be assessed, though, before you say your child has a learning difference. Make sure there are no medically-based issues, such as physical hearing loss or vision problems. These problems require specialized attention so learning can take place effectively. Note also that some children develop a bit slower than their peers.

A *learning difference* reflects *how a child prefers to learn best.* If a child is determined to have a *learning difference*, it is *not grounds for receiving special education* services of support. When a child has a *learning disability*, it demonstrates that the child *cannot meet grade-level standards, requires special education services*, and *is eligible for an Individualized Education Program (IEP).*

The **DSM-V** (Diagnostic and Statistical Manual of Mental Disorders) is a set of guidelines that psychologists and school psychologists in the United States use to diagnose individuals whose development differs from the norm. The DSM-V identifies a "Learning Disability" as being anything from dyslexia (reading fluency or comprehension) to dyscalculia (math problem-solving).

Specific Learning Disability (SLD) exists as one of the thirteen categories of classifications provided under the Federal Individual with Disabilities Education Act (IDEA), for children three to twenty-one years of age.

IDEA guarantees a free appropriate public education (FAPE) be made available in the least restrictive environment (LRE). Under IDEA, however, there is no classification for Learning Difference.

"Learning Difference" is not a diagnostic term, and doesn't usually appear in a neuro-psychological/psycho-educational evaluation or on an Individual Education Plan (IEP).

So, if your child is identified as being a child with learning differences, there may be no supports and services provided under IDEA. Accommodations can be made under a 504 plan, which refers to Section 504 of the Rehabilitation Act and the American with Disabilities Act. (This 504 Plan will be discussed later in this chapter.)

Several Additional Red Flags you may notice may include difficulties with:

- *Affect* – doesn't smile, seems depressed, or unhappy
- *Attention disorder* – can't seem to sit still or is lethargic
- *Auditory processing* – has nothing physically wrong with his hearing, but cannot understand auditory information. He may take time to respond to questions
- *Learning* – doesn't seem to "catch on" by ordinary means of providing directions and learning, and needs different ways of teaching
- *Listening* – doesn't seem to follow directions or understand what is said

- *Movement* – difficulties balancing, walking, skipping, and/or running

- *Sensory processing* – cannot organize his body to integrate sensory information properly, which affects appropriate responses to the environment (i.e., has aversion to sounds, which become overwhelming, and he needs a quiet place where he can "reduce the overstimulation of sounds and movements" that other children seem to be able to tolerate). A sensory processing difficulty is not a "stand-alone" service, so if your child has that difficulty, he would also have to exhibit a special education classification

- *Social emotional learning* – can't seem to regulate emotions (i.e., worried, anxious, lashes out at others)

- *Social skills* – difficulty joining groups, making friends, keeping friends; feels left out or would rather be alone; difficulty keeping a conversation going

- *Thinking skills* – has a hard time solving problems

There is no worse feeling than for a child, of any age, to feel different, unlikeable, and misunderstood by his teacher and his peers—simply because of the way he was born or the way he learns. No child should have to struggle to learn.

When Your Gut Speaks – Act!

As parents, you "know" when your child is learning differently. You can "feel it" in your gut. The best thing you can do is act early! One of the best bits of advice you can follow, and one that the Centers for Disease Control also preaches, is: *Learn the Signs and Act Early!*

Early intervention is one of the greatest gifts you can give your children. By providing intervention, you are not merely stimulating the brain; you are structuring the brain. The formative years for brain development are from birth to five years of age. Providing services and support can bring your child from helplessness to confidence and from despair to joy at any age. Learning does not have to stop at age five. The latest brain research shows us that we keep learning until we die. So, you're *never too old* to learn!

Sometimes, parents do not want to admit there is a problem with their child. For some, it is emotional. They feel like they are a bad parent, or blame their spouse for the problem. Others experience denial. If they don't deal with the red flag, maybe it will go away. So, they take a "wait and see" attitude. They don't want to put their child into therapy or get a tutor. They think, *Maybe he'll outgrow his awkwardness. Maybe he will stop hitting other children.* However, once a red flag is seen and an area identified, it's important you act quickly, purposefully, and consistently. Your child's well-being depends on it—as does yours!

Examine Your Children's Hearts, not Their Behavior

Imagine the morning alarm going off for another day of school. Instead of being happy and confident about greeting a new day, seeing friends in class, playing on the playground, and learning new things, your child feels anxious, angry, resentful, withdrawn, upset, or lethargic about going to school one more day.

Your child may wake up late for school. Whatever you do to encourage him to get up on time, he finds every excuse to wear you down. He can't find his toothbrush—the same one that's put away in the same spot night after night. Or, he can't seem to put his shoe on the right foot—although he has done that correctly a hundred times before, especially when he's getting ready to go to his favorite ice cream store with his grandma!

When he hugs his sister, he gives her a skin burn around her neck. Was it because your child meant to hurt her, or was it that he couldn't control his own strength? If your child begins pushing on you before bedtime, and he continues to push, is it to hurt you, or is it because he is seeking deep pressure before bedtime?

Listen to the words your child uses. Watch behaviors. He may be the child who was perfectly fine driving to school with you, but once the car pulled onto the school grounds, it's as if the "devil" has gotten into him. He starts to scream and shriek. He says, "I am not going into school!" He yells, "I hate school, and everybody there!"; "I hate my teacher who is always picking on me!"; "I hate my classmates who take the teacher's side!"

What is the heart of your child telling you? Is your child being oppositional? Is he being defiant? Is he showing you his distress? Is he telling you that something deeper is happening that doesn't feel quite right inside him? Is he really asking for your help?

Actions Speak Louder than Words

In a parent survey, many parents commented about being met with hostility from the school administrator and classroom teacher when they mentioned something was different about their child and they wanted an assessment. Some parents were told, "There is nothing wrong with your child," or "Don't worry, he'll get over it!" Other parents commented that the school was wonderful and met their child's needs and their own.

When you see the signs and signals, do not be afraid to act. If your child is aged three years or older, put a request in writing for an evaluation at your child's home school. If your child is younger, check out local early intervention programs and have your child assessed. Many parents do not know that their child can be assessed before kindergarten. Early intervention services are available for eligible children aged birth through three years, and school services can start at age three or earlier.

Once an assessment has been requested in writing, with your signed signature, an assessment must take place within forty-five days. Then, a meeting will be held fourteen days after the assessment to determine the IFSP (Individualized Family Service Plan) for children birth through three years of age, or an IEP (Individualized Education Program) for children three years or older. The meeting must take place to go over the test results, and to see if your child is eligible for special education services.

If your child does not qualify for special education services but you see the difference in your child, visit your child's healthcare professional whenever you are in doubt. Ask for a screening and/ or referral to outside sources (i.e., speech-language pathologist, occupational therapist, physical therapist, etc.) who can assess your child.

Sometimes, a child's difference may not affect his educational learning, and may not be severe enough to warrant special education. Your child's difference may be seen as a medical necessity or an area that is not impacting his learning— nonetheless, it warrants intervention.

504s to the Rescue

For children who do not qualify for special education, but need accommodations to help them succeed in school, there are also 504 plans. School districts can provide a 504 plan for your child, and as a parent you can request it. The 504 plan comes from Section 504 of the Rehabilitation Act and the American with Disabilities Act. Unlike an IEP, specific academic goals, benchmarks, and baseline data are not included in a 504 plan. Accommodations are included to help your child participate in class and succeed in a general education classroom. It is a good idea to have a 504 in writing, so you are sure what the accommodations are for your child.

Various accommodations may include, but are not limited to:

- Providing your child with an FM system in the classroom
- Placing your child at the front of the classroom, or in a location in the classroom where he can see the teacher's face and lips
- Requesting and/or requiring teachers and aides receive training in your child's particular difference(s) (e.g., webinars, videos, YouTubes, lectures about ADHD, or sensory processing challenges, auditory processing, etc.)
- Providing a child with extra time for test-taking
- Providing a quiet space, for test-taking
- Providing a space solely for your child, with no other students, when taking a test
- Providing a quiet place for doing homework
- Providing a tutor after school to help with assignments
- Providing your child with someone who can take notes for him in class
- Providing a special chair for balancing and sitting
- Providing special grips for holding pencils
- Providing technological support

The 504 plan can be a good tool that helps your child receive the instruction he needs inside the classroom. It can make a significant difference in your child's learning experience. If you think your child may benefit from a few accommodations, ask about them at your school. You will learn more about how this worked in Carson's success story in Chapter 10.

Get a Sense of Belonging

Learning differences can make your child feel excluded, academically and socially, by his peers—and also by his teacher. You, as a parent, can also feel excluded as you get looks from other parents.

To reduce these negative feelings, see if you are able to:

- Volunteer in your child's classroom
- Observe your child to see how he is doing in class
- Volunteer as a member of the parent association
- Volunteer as an officer of your parent association
- Run for an office on the school board

Be valuable to your child's teacher and school, so you can have input for school and classroom operations.

Select Professional(s) Carefully

Once you see a sign, you may begin looking for a professional who can serve your child's needs. Do you want to go to a clinic, or do you want the therapist to go to your home? Does your child need a professional who is matter-of-fact, or one who is gentle and kind? Do you know your own budget? What can you afford? Will your insurance company pay for your child's therapy?

One of the worst things you can do is keep trying out new therapists, or have multiple therapists working on the same goals. This can confuse your child when two people have different approaches. Make sure the therapists speak with one another so each one knows what the other is doing. There will probably be enough for them both to do without confusing your child. But communication is paramount. You know your child best. Often, you may have to try different professionals until you get the "right fit." The therapist will be your child's booster, confidante, and friend. Choose wisely.

Just Because I Have a Difference Doesn't Mean I'm Stupid

For Alex's mother, Jewel, the "red flags" were present. She didn't know what she was seeing, but she knew something wasn't right. She had a rough time raising her twins, with double demands. As described in the beginning anecdote, Alex's lack of attention had gotten the best of him. He wasn't able to finish his assignments. It would have been better to have him take his work home to finish it and let him play outside with his classmates. Alex needed to release the stressors that had crept into his body. He was aware he hadn't completed his assignment and was being penalized because of it.

Alex was sinking fast. He didn't like school and was only in the second grade. He had a teacher who felt no compassion for him and his learning difference. The teacher just wanted him to fit into her classroom. That wasn't going to happen, because Alex was already showing signs of Attention Deficit Hyperactivity Disorder (ADHD). His mother had taken Alex to see a doctor for his ADHD symptoms, and although Jewel didn't believe in giving her child any drugs, she would have given him the prescribed medication to ease him through his suffering, mood swings, and depression. However, Alex refused to take the drug because he didn't like how it made him feel. He said it made him feel worse!

Jewel searched and prayed for over a year that she would find someone who could help her son. Alex didn't want to feel different, and yet that is how he felt. Just because he had ADHD didn't mean he was stupid.

Searching for the 'Perfect' Therapist

After a year of searching and trying different therapists, Jewel got a recommendation about a therapist from another parent she had met in a Parent Teacher's Group. She called the therapist and the therapist had room for Alex. Alex was suspicious of therapists, having been to so many in a variety of different settings, offices, hospitals, and clinics. This therapist used a room attached to her own home. The atmosphere was relaxed and not so "clinical" as a doctor's office.

This therapist understood Alex's skepticism, after being to so many specialists with poor results. The therapist specifically invited a girl from Alex's class, who was receiving therapy from her, to switch her usual therapy time for one day. When Alex arrived, he would see her coming out of the therapy room before he got to go in. This compassionate therapist knew that Alex thought he was so different from the other kids in his class. Perhaps when he saw a girl he knew from his very own class coming out of the therapy room, he would know he wasn't alone and wouldn't feel so helpless and misunderstood.

The setup worked! Alex couldn't believe his classmate was going for therapy, too. This signaled to Alex that he wasn't alone! This signaled to his mother that she wasn't alone, either. She had found a compassionate therapist who understood her son and his journey. She was grateful. When Alex went back to school, he recognized his classmate was like him, and a new friendship was born.

A Teacher's Caring Heart Makes a Difference

A teacher can make or ruin your child's day, and possibly life. For your child who is different, the way a teacher talks to him, includes him, and understands him can generate a day filled with confidence and joy or a day that brings him down. Teachers are busy with core curriculum standards they must include in every overcrowded class, so it is a wonder if your child's teacher has time to know your child and teach them in a way that is most beneficial to his differences.

Alex's twin sister, Rosie, could finish assignments, contributed to the class, and did well once she was in school. Each morning, she would have a panic attack with thoughts of "not being good enough." She hated the idea of saying goodbye to her mother in the car, and would scream at the top of her lungs. It took all her mother's patience to get Rosie out of the car so she could be walked to class. Rosie was eight years old—too old to have her mother walk her to class, and too old to have panic attacks.

A teacher's caring heart turned Rosie around. Rosie's mother told her teacher, Ms. Robertson, that Rosie was having a hard time getting out of the car without having a screaming fit and a meltdown. Rosie's teacher knew that Rosie was really a good kind-hearted child who liked to help others and feel important (what child doesn't want to feel important?). Once Rosie was in class, she did well with her studies.

So, Ms. Robertson thought of how she could help Rosie get out of the car each morning without having a panic attack. Ms. Robertson decided she would give Rosie a job that would give her a reason to get to school on time, get out of the car each morning without a meltdown, and make her feel important. Rosie was entrusted with the job of walking Ms. Robertson's five-year-old daughter from Rosie's classroom down to the kindergarten classroom. It was a win-win for both Rosie and Ms. Robertson.

Rosie felt special! Mrs. Robertson had her daughter delivered to her kindergarten classroom by a competent student. Rosie didn't scream anymore in the car, and even urged her mother to get to school earlier. Rosie had a purpose to get to her classroom. She was now the personal escort for Mrs. Robertson's daughter—an important job indeed.

When the signs and signals appear, does your child have a teacher who is compassionate and will *go the extra mile* to make your child feel important and special, each and every day? Rosie became more confident and joyful having a reason to get to school each day. Do you have a Ms. Robertson in your child's life? If not, what would it take to find one?

Reflections

1. Is my child showing any red flags that sets him apart from other children his age?

2. Do I know the steps I need to take to have my child evaluated by early intervention, at school, or by a private therapist?

3. Does my child's healthcare professional have the ability to write a prescription for my child to be tested, and does my healthcare plan have the services he will need?

4. Have I made sure I checked the background of the person who is going to assess my child, and has the assessor conducted many tests and/or offered much therapy to a child like mine?

5. Are there other parents I know who have also used this professional(s) who might give me a glowing recommendation?

6

Jump-Start Your Child's Confidence and Joy

Juanita is an eight-year-old girl who is on the Autism Spectrum and has Attention Deficit Hyperactive Disorder. She has limited eye gaze except when she looks in the mirror to brush her long black hair. She hates going to school since she has no friends. She spends time playing by herself. Her teacher tries to invite Juanita to join her classmates on the playground, but Juanita prefers to be alone. Her parents had hoped Juanita would like a sport or a school subject so she could excel and be confident and joyful.

Juanita's talents are not clear cut. Her parents had to think long and hard to figure out, "What does she do that makes her happy?" Juanita's parents saw how much their daughter's face lit up every time she saw a dog, She would let the dog lick her hand as it wagged its tail. She became excited and happy, and began speaking to the puppy. She threw a ball to a neighbor's dog and said, "Bring it here, Red!" Her speech was usually unclear, but when speaking to the dog, her speech was clear as can be.

Juanita's parents decided that having a puppy could be just what "the doctor ordered," After many trips to various kennels and shelters, "Kisses" arrived. "Kisses," a Goldendoodle, was the perfect dog for Juanita. It was kind and gentle, and an excellent family dog. It was also easy to train, and a good match for a first-time or timid owner. Juanita was in heaven. As she sat down on the family couch, "Kisses" would lie down right next to her as they watched television together. Goldendoodles don't shed much. They need to be brushed regularly to remove dead and dying hair, and prevent matting. Juanita, who loved brushing her own hair, now loved to brush "Kisses'" hair. She took a big interest in the Goldendoodle breed, grooming her dog, and taking "Kisses" outside for walks with her mother.

Juanita can now see herself, one day, becoming a veterinarian or animal shelter worker. Juanita feels the love of her dog, with whom she's bonded and connected. She is a happier child, and looks forward to going to school now, because she knows what will be waiting for her when she returns home... the wet kisses of her precious dog, a wagging tail greeting her at the door, and, most importantly, unconditional love.

All Children Have Unique Talents

Talent is an innate ability or a natural endowment. Sometimes, talent is hidden. Other times, talent sparkles for all to see. Often, a child with learning differences may not be able to notice his own talent. He may feel excluded in school because of his lack of academic success, and be extremely upset because he has no friends. Or perhaps he is looking at his brother, who is a star on a soccer team. Or maybe he sees his cousin able to ride a bicycle, when he still can't seem to find out how to balance himself on one. Maybe he doesn't recognize his own skills and talents.

What are some of the talents your child may have? Art, music, dance, sports, or crafts? Hiking or the outdoors, computer skills or number computations, academic expertise, or entrepreneurship or helping others—including pets, like Juanita?

Talents build confidence and joy. As an adult, you feel special when you have a talent. You feel confident that there is something you can do that others may not. You may be acknowledged by others for having unique talents, and then you may acknowledge yourself. Children with learning differences are not any different. They tend to thrive when they realize they have their own talents and can succeed.

How do you figure out what talent or talents your child has? You can look at what comes easily to your child. See if that talent brings your child joy. Although adults may search to find out what their talents are and what brings them happiness, your child may lack insight about himself. It will be up to you to provide opportunities for your child to explore his own uniqueness.

Talent Identifier 101

As a parent of a child with learning differences, you need to identify a talent your child has—something that makes him happy. As a parent, you want your child to be liked. You want your child to have friends. You want your child to feel confident. You want your child to experience joy. You want your child to succeed.

As a parent, you know your child best. What brings him a feeling of being special and of belonging? To play an active role in jump-starting your child's talent or talents, it will be up to you to take a good, long look at your child. What comes to your child easier than anyone else in the family? Perhaps you don't need a long look, because you have already noticed those "ah ha moments" when you may have thought, *Oh, wow, look at him do that!* Or you may have said out loud, "Way to go!"

Perhaps you have seen your child engage in an activity or activities with great skill, ease, and delight. Did you ever notice that your child with a learning difference is:

- A great skateboarder who can zoom down the street with great ease?
- A bicycle rider extraordinaire, maneuvering his way along the pathway at your local beach, park, or neighborhood street, with perfect balance?
- An Olympian swimmer, racing to the end of the pool in record speed?
- A super water polo player?
- A fantastic tennis player?
- A successful bowler, who can make some strikes and spares?
- Great with pets, like Juanita?
- Extremely gentle and kind, and loves to help others?
- A budding artist who draws pictures like no other?
- An exceptional designer of clothes and jewelry?
- An entrepreneur, with skills for company building? (lemonade stands included)
- A super potter who can create ceramic masterpieces?
- A great chess player?
- A super musician?
- A graceful dancer?
- A superb number cruncher?
- An Einstein scientist in the making?
- A future Academy Award-winning actor like _____?
- A melodious singer?
- A future space explorer?
- A mechanic who loves to take things apart and put them back together?
- An awesome financial wizard?
- A _____ (fill in the blank)?

Mission Possible

The mission set before you is to notice the intricacies of what makes your child happy, or what challenges your child. Be intentional. Notice what your child with learning differences is good at and seeks out. Notice what your child seems to withdraw from, couldn't be bothered with, and makes excuses for why he doesn't want to engage in that activity.

Watch your child. Observe him during his daily activities. Listen to the words he is using. See when he smiles. See what he can't wait to do. Put a *spotlight* on your child. Make a list of the skills and talents you notice your child displays. You need to fully recognize what stands out about your child. What can he do that is different from others? What is he willing to try?

At the same time, make a list about what makes your child uncomfortable. What things make him nervous? What things make him embarrassed? What does he absolutely not want to engage in? What seems to be a challenge for him? What is he not willing to try?

Following are some questions to ask yourself. Be sure to write down your answers:

6 Simple Questions – What Makes My Child Happy?

- What does my child look forward to?
- What brings a smile to my child's face?
- What is my child always ready to do—anytime, anywhere?
- What does my child always talk about that he likes to do?
- What makes my child get up with a smile on his face, knowing he is doing that activity that day?
- What does my child continue to enjoy after many weeks and months?

6 Simple Questions – What Makes My Child Unhappy?

- What is my child challenged by?
- What does my child refuse to do or even try?
- What does my child stay away from, even when others are encouraging him?
- What does my child seem afraid of?
- What brings tears to my child's eyes just from mentioning it?
- What does my child always say "no" to doing?

Your intention is to discover your child's talent, or areas that can lend themselves to your child developing a talent. A child who demonstrates talents is confident, joyful, and successful. He can have others drawn to him, make friends, and belong. A child who sees himself as having no talents or special gifts may feel dejected, isolated, and friendless.

Following are nine simple questions you can ask your child:

- What activities, hobbies, etc., do you look forward to doing?
- What activities are easy for you to do?
- What activities make you happy?
- What activities make you feel nervous?
- What activities make you feel embarrassed?
- What activities don't you ever want to do again?
- What activities make you uncomfortable?
- What activities make you scared and unsure of yourself?
- What activities do you want to do over and over again, and why?

Additional Talent Detectives

You are not the only one who engages with your child. Others may know your child through their experiences. How are your child's talents seen through the eyes of your child's...

- Teacher (pre-school, elementary, middle school, high school, etc.)
- Tutor
- Therapist
- Librarian
- Medical Healthcare Professional
- Extended Family Members
- Babysitter
- Camp Counselor
- Religious Leader/Counselor
- Family Friends
- Coach
- _____ (fill in the blank)

Your child may show a different side of him to these people. In the classroom, for example, the teacher may have noticed what a great singer your child is, while at home he doesn't sing at all. Or perhaps the religious leader noticed how kind and loving your child is to other children, while at home he is his sister's worst nightmare.

Mindfully Encourage Skills and Talents

Sometimes you may think your child loves a certain activity, only to find out that he appeared to love it because he thought you loved it and he wanted to please you. Likewise, he may appear to love an activity because his sister or brother loves it.

Sort out the likes and the dislikes your child feels and/or expresses. See if your child's answers match up to your own.

By witnessing the unfolding of your child's talents and noticing your child's passion, you learn more about what makes your child "tick" and how to support your child's success.

After you've figured out what makes your child happy and what talents he has, you may find that a support plan is needed. Your child may love to play the violin, but you don't know one musical note from another. Seek community resources. Discover camps, classes, and coaches who can build your child's talents. Increase your child's comfort level so he is supported and "shines" (learn more about this in Chapter 9).

Positive Reinforcers

After finding out about your child's talents and what motivates him, excites him, and pleases him, you may need some additional strategies to keep your child going, boost him up, and increase his talents. You want to be positive and find ways that support your child and encourage him.

Using a positive reinforcer is a way you can reinforce a response, and one that your child will continue in the future. Examples of positive reinforcers are:

Praise

- *Be process oriented with your praise.* You don't just want to tell your child, "Good job!" That does not praise the process of how he got to do the "good job." For example, if the talent you've noticed that your child demonstrates is being an extraordinary bicycle rider, maneuvering his way along the pathway with perfect balance, then you will want to praise the process by saying, "I liked how you got your bicycle out of the garage, took your time to get on it before you began to pedal along the pathway, and stayed up on the bicycle the whole ride."

- *Be specific with your praise.* Reinforcing a response leads to the probability that the response will re-occur in the future. So, if dance is the talent your child demonstrates, you might say, "Your pirouettes are so graceful, and your rhythm is perfectly timed with the music!"

- *Be sincere and genuine with your praise.* Your child can tell when you really mean what you say, or if you are just saying something without meaning it. Look at your child when you give praise. Make eye contact, and smile.

Rewards

- *Physical rewards.* Set out the rules. "After you bike ride for five laps around the park, you can go to the store for a yogurt with sprinkles."

- *Stickers.* "When you practice your violin each day for _# minutes [amount of time], you will get _# of stickers." When your child reaches a certain agreed upon number of stickers, your child trades them in to buy a game at the store, get an ice cream sundae, get time on his tablet, etc.

- *Token rewards* for older children. Every time they complete their skill practice, they receive a token. After they have received a certain number of tokens, they exchange the token rewards for prizes (think Chuck E. Cheese's or Dave & Buster's) or privileges.

Charts

- *Hang up a chart on the wall* for your child to see. Place happy faces, stars, or stickers of your child's choice on the chart for completing the practice.

- *When your child* gets the agreed upon number of stickers, your child earns agreed upon reward, or a reward of his choice (i.e., going to a favorite amusement park, visiting a favorite restaurant or relative, etc.).

Hugs

- *Touch is a human sense* that sends messages of affection, appreciation, and love.

- *Giving hugs to your child* for doing well and "hanging in there" sends messages of warmth, caring, and tenderness.

Kind Words

- *When you know that your child has attempted something* even though he was afraid of it, you can tell him, "I know you were afraid to go rock wall climbing. I like how you climbed up the wall and rang the bell, even though you were scared."

- *Also try phrases like these:* "You always make my day when I see you being a team player throwing the ball to Billie on your team," or "I love how you ran around the bases and slid into home plate!"

Self-Affirmations

- *Have your child say something* aloud and positive, using the present tense as if it has already happened (e.g., "I am _____", "I am a great rock climber", or "I am a caring friend").

- *Self-affirmations affect neurochemistry* and well-being.

- *Saying a positive self-affirmation aloud daily*, and believing it, can build self-confidence and boost your child's positive feelings about himself.

Celebrations

- *Celebrate* your child's achievements.

- *Have a party* and ask your child to give you input as to what kind of party he wants.

- *Get some ice cream* with sprinkles and cookie dough toppings as a treat for your child, or whatever your child enjoys, for playing on the soccer team and giving it his all, singing in the choir, dancing in the recital, or helping needy children. If ice cream is not his favorite, then find out what is and celebrate with popcorn, doughnuts, or a party at an activity park.

Creating a Safe Place

Your child feels good about himself when he achieves. He becomes proud of his own talents, and skills. He is confident and joyful when he is successful. As a parent, you feel better too—especially when you see your child's confidence and joy soar, and he is accepted and included in activities.

When your child feels confident and successful, the team, school, camp, or other organization feels inviting, comforting, and safe. Your child has found a "happy place," filled with acceptance and love. It's like being in a family away from home.

Savoring these feelings empowers your child's strengths and skills, and provides greater opportunities for continued success.

Be Your Child's Biggest Fan

When you discover your child's talent, be prepared to go the extra mile for whatever it takes to make your child happy and witness your child's confidence and joy. Lila, a nine-year-old girl with visual problems and muscle tics, loved being in the pool, splashing around and having fun. When her school opened up trials for joining the water polo team, Lila was the first to have her mother, Charlene, sign her up. Charlene knew her daughter loved the water, but didn't realize how much. When she saw her daughter try out for the team and make it, Charlene realized how much determination, stamina, and love for the water Lila really had.

The only thing is that when your child is on the water polo team, and has to be in the pool at 6:00 a.m., Monday through Friday, you have to wake up early, too, no matter how unappealing!

Being your child's *biggest* fan is a full-time commitment. Day after day, you have to find your own stamina to support your child's efforts. You've encouraged your daughter to get out of bed, even when she felt like sleeping in. You've watched your daughter become part of a team. You've seen her being accepted, valued, and contributing to her teammates, as much as they have contributed to her.

Then one day, after all of your daughter's effort, perseverance, and questioning about her own abilities on the team, you witness your child's confidence and joy soar. Your daughter's water polo team had been invited to play in a Statewide Water Polo Competition. As part of the Nationwide invitation, a USA Olympian Female Water Polo Champion spoke to your daughter's team. She told about her own *learning difference*, and how her mother supported her to do her best. This Olympian inspired Lila and her teammates to strive for excellence, and collaborate with one another, sparking them to play with greater determination and camaraderie. Charlene continued being her daughter's *biggest fan*, and cheered Lila and her team on.

To the delight of all in attendance, Lila and her team won the National Championship for girls aged 8-10. Lila experienced more confidence and joy than she had ever felt before. Lila also felt good about her own performance, being accepted by others, and being part of a team. Charlene was glad that her daughter discovered a sport she loved, and had not given up. Charlene was glad that she had not given up either!

Yes, *you* are your child's **biggest fan**!

Consistent and Sustainable – Way to Go!

All successful people will tell you that it takes consistency and perseverance to achieve.

When you look at your child's talents, you may wonder what it will take to be consistent and sustain the skills that promote confidence and joy. Following are some questions you may ask:

- *Long-term value* – What value does your child get from this talent?
- *Authentic purpose* – Is your child happy, and does the skill come from within?
- *Constant and consistent sense of focus* – Can your child focus on the goals and be constant and consistent? (Can you be, too?)
- *Strong emotional engagement* – Does your child have a strong emotional engagement with the demonstrated skill?
- *Continuous growth, innovation, and striving* – Does your child grow continually in this activity?
- *Community* – Can you identify a community where your child's likes, interests, and talents are valued?

As a parent, you invest in your child's capabilities. You encourage him. You value him. You contribute to his success. Often, this may mean that you are spending your own time and money to get him where he needs to go. But it is all worthwhile when your child feels *confident, joyful, and successful.*

Reflections

1. Can you make a list of activities you have noticed that are a challenge to your child, and a list of activities that give your child a sense of joy and happiness?

2. Have you asked your child which activity(ies) he finds the most joyful while he is engaged in it (and may bring others benefits, too)?

3. Which activity can you begin to explore with your child?

4. Is there a list of steps you can write down that you need to take to sign your child up to be on a team, register for a class, attend a camp, or enroll in a school in the area of his talent?

5. Are there other parents you know who you may contact to find out more about various activities—whose child may be enrolled in an upcoming group activity that your child can join, too?

7

Going to Bat for Your Child: Parents as Advocates

Ella loved preschool. Now, as a second grader, she does not like school at all. Ella is really struggling to learn to read and spell, and feels very different from her peers. There were red flags in kindergarten when she couldn't grasp the pre-reading skills. Her parents started advocating for her at that time, requesting extra assistance at school as well as testing to determine if she was eligible for any other types of services. Her parents were advised to "give it time and she will catch up," but that didn't happen.

By the middle of first grade, Ella had slipped further behind with her achievement and started to have anxiety about going to school. Every morning she would have "meltdowns" before leaving her house and refuse to go into the classroom. Her parents met with the teacher and learned that all students in the class were participating in a supplemental computer-based reading program in which students advanced based on their reading skill achievement. Ella's difficulty with reading had prevented her from advancing. Her parents learned that Ella had failed the same level forty-seven times and still was not advancing.

Her parents were quite upset, knowing this had been allowed to happen without their being told. Now, they understood the reason for the daily meltdowns and anxiety. They went into action. They knew they had to really go to bat for Ella, and that they did! They identified professional resources to assist in getting a "game plan" together, requested a meeting with the educational team at Ella's school, formed "team Ella," had testing done to determine the cause of her reading disability, and implemented a plan and strategies to ensure Ella's learning success and ultimately Ella's confidence and joy.

As the benefits of her parents' advocacy have fallen into place, Ella has become happier and more confident, and the anxiety and daily meltdowns have disappeared.

Advocating for Your Child: What Parents Need to Know

Parents of kids with differences *must* advocate for their child. You may be thinking, *I already know this. I already advocate for my child... tell me something I* don't *know!* Well, here are a few things you may not know:

- Advocating is a tough duty when done the right way
- Advocating can make you really uncomfortable at times
- Advocating pushes your limits
- Advocating is exhausting
- Advocating can "rock some boats"
- Advocating is time-consuming

On the bright side:

- Advocating can be rewarding
- Advocating can build relationships

- Advocating can bring your child success, confidence, and joy
- Advocating can make change happen
- Advocating can help others learn from you
- Advocating is action- and results-oriented
- Advocating is empowering
- Advocating opens lines of communication

So, advocating for your child is an involved process that should be done strategically and with specific purpose and intent... and it will keep you on your toes.

Other than parents, who else advocates for children who are different or struggling? Of course, there are various parent groups who work tirelessly to advocate for the rights of children with *special needs*. But do keep in mind that not all children who are different are special needs. Any child who is *different* and may be struggling in school is going to need someone to go to bat for them. That someone is their mom or dad, or both. But there are also counselors, therapists such as speech-language, occupational, and behavioral therapists, physicians, teachers, and special educators, as well as coaches. But no matter the number of professionals advocating for your child, no one will be as concerned, passionate, and thorough as you are.

You know your child better than anyone else. Though your child may spend six plus hours in school each day, you *know* your child. You know your child's strengths, weaknesses, and challenges. You know what makes him/her happy, what brings joy, what robs joy, what builds confidence, what robs confidence, what causes frustration, what inspires learning, and what turns learning off. You know what makes your child tick. So, despite the good intentions of others who are involved in your child's life, you are the one who can help to identify and push for the activities, opportunities, resources, and people your child needs to succeed.

It's not just about success. It's about building your child's confidence and joy so they *can* succeed. The previous chapters addressed the importance of confidence and joy as well as awareness of confidence and joy robbers. So, as you are pushing for resources or making sure the rights of your child are in place, keep in mind that the underlying purpose of advocacy efforts is to protect and maintain your child's confidence and joy so he/she can feel good about achievement and success.

Parents as Heroes

There's no question that parents who tirelessly go to bat for their children are heroes. Heroes are people admired for courage, outstanding achievements, or noble qualities. Never underestimate the advocacy work you are doing. You are heroes in the eyes of your child, other parents, and the professionals who work with your child. You are admired by so many for your courage when you feel like you are always going against the flow or bucking the system. You show up at meetings that can be uncomfortable or difficult. You ask for services or resources for your child that no one would ever ask for. You make the impossible possible. You create opportunities and environments that build your child's sense of success and confidence. You create teams and communities of support for your child. You are sometimes so focused that you don't see all your accomplishments for your child. But they are there. You have done so much for your child solely for the purpose of making the world right, fair, equitable, and success-oriented, without realizing that you are building in systems to ensure that he/she will experience confidence and joy just like every other child.

Learning to Advocate

Parents are not born with advocacy skills. Just about every parent can learn the skills necessary to be an effective advocate for their child. Advocating doesn't have to solely be the parent's responsibility. You will have to be proactive to make sure that your child's needs are met within the family, at school, socially, in clubs or recreational activities, and ultimately in the community. When you realize that your child's needs are not being met and no one is really stepping up to bat for your child, that's the "ah ha" moment for you. That's the moment when you shift your thinking from, *I'm just the mom/dad/parent,* to *I'm my child's advocate.* This shift in thinking can be empowering, and is essential in making sure that your child will be getting what is needed for achievement, success, confidence, and happiness.

Where to Begin

As parents, you may not know where to start in the advocacy process. You do know for sure that your child is not achieving because you have already had parent-teacher conferences, feedback from parents or other adults, or have had your own experiences where concerns about your child have been shared or observed. Perhaps the school is recommending a student study team (SST) or formal testing for eligibility for an Individualized Education Plan (IEP). Maybe there have been "red flags" or general concerns about achievement academically or socially. A lack of achievement can be a child who is just not learning to read, spell, or do math and falls below grade-level expectations, or a child who cannot get their classwork done and has to stay in at recess to get the work completed. This, by the way, is a common practice in school—but really is a punishment for a child with learning challenges or who processes at a slower rate of speed. Every child needs recess to move, have a break, or experience the fresh air. Denying a child recess is a huge confidence and joy robber, and a reason for a parent to jump in and advocate for their child.

So, when parents put on the hat of "advocate," they often are asking themselves, *What do I do first?* A sensible first step is to find people in your community who can provide you with information and support. First-time advocate parents may feel intimidated, inexperienced, or uninformed when meeting with their child's educational team by themselves. So, having an experienced support person to coach, guide, or even attend a meeting can be helpful and assist you in building effective and productive relationships and outcomes.

Gaining Support in Your Advocacy Efforts

Who or what are support persons? Support persons are often other parents who have experience advocating for their own children. They can serve as your mentor or coach to assist you in navigating the complexities of educational or healthcare systems. Support persons can also include a physician, counselor, or family member who also has experience in dealing with these complicated systems.

So, what specifically can a support person do for you? First, they will *listen* to you—really listen to your story, issues, concerns, and obstacles. They will provide you with the appropriate and necessary information you need to address your concerns, and help you develop a plan to move forward to find solutions. Your support person can help you understand how the different processes and systems work and what you and your child's rights are. But most importantly, this person will provide you with the moral and emotional support you will need navigating the rough terrain.

Building Relationships Through the Advocacy Process

Once you have your support person in place, you should start working on building relationships with all the people you will interact with. Advocating can be contentious, but it doesn't have to be. Developing and refining your "relationship-building" skills can make you an effective and respected advocate. From the beginning to the end of the advocacy process, it is always necessary to be polite, kind, and respectful of others. Just these three qualities will go quite a long way in building positive relationships. Your advocacy efforts are going to be more successful if you can build positive and mutually beneficial relationships with those individuals you will be "negotiating" with. Be patient and actively listen to what others have to say, and be receptive to hearing their perspective. When sitting around a table, everyone wants to be heard and come to agreement about what is necessary, fair, and possible for a child who has unique needs. Making demands and declaring "rights" doesn't work, and does nothing for relationship-building. Being flexible in your interactions, discussions, negotiations, and decisions as you work to find solutions for your child will go a long way in relationship-building and ultimately getting what your child needs for success, happiness, and confidence.

Those Meetings!

You should always be informed, prepared, and organized when attending meetings concerning your child. Present information in a calm but matter-of-fact manner, and keep it organized and easy-to-understand. Provide others with all information that will be helpful throughout the process of problem-solving for your child. You are always encouraged to ask questions when meeting with educational experts or the educational team. Let's say, for example, you are attending an IEP meeting and are discussing a recommendation for dealing with your child's reading problem. The educational team may offer a recommendation for an intervention you know won't be helpful because you have done your homework investigating appropriate reading interventions. You might ask, "Does this program have research data behind it, and what can you tell me about it?"

Another question may be, "How does this program compare to other reading programs?" Finish off with something like, "Can you tell me/us why your school recommends this particular program?" By asking questions, you are able to have an interactive discussion in a friendly and non-confrontational way. You are basically saying, "I want to hear what you have to say," which is important in building relationships. Positive relationships between you and the educational team will only benefit your child.

Building a Support Team When Advocating

Another important step for advocating parents is to build a team of support and success for your child. Who should be on this team? The most effective teams are made up of parents, the teacher, any therapist such as a speech-language therapist, a counselor if the child and family has a counselor, a tutor, and a special educator if a child is receiving special education services. Why a team? Teams are collaborative and are working toward the same goal for the child with learning differences: achievement and success. Each team member has a unique and special purpose with shared outcomes. It is essential that when a child has so many people working for and with him/ her there is shared information, expectations, understandings, and strategies. When all the team members are "on the same page," only great things can happen for your child. Keep in mind that everyone who is on the team is really busy taking care of other kids, so having a team doesn't necessarily mean that they have to plan and schedule formal team meetings. This type of formality is time-consuming and for the most part unrealistic given everyone's busy schedule. Someone needs to take the lead and be the "team leader," setting up a system for communicating with the entire team.

Outcomes for your child are only as good as how effective and accountable the team is. The concept of a team outside the educational team dedicated to a child's success is not that common, so setting up how the team will work together is really important. Parents should politely and respectfully assert the need for a team, then agree who is on the team and how the team is accountable for reaching measurable and attainable outcomes for your child. Nothing sucks the life out of a child more than lack of achievement and success. A high performing team ensures your child's achievement and success is essential to his/her well-being. Achievement makes a child feel successful, and success makes a child happy and confident. So, get your team in place!

Know What You Want for Your Child

Once you have identified your support person, built positive relationships, and assembled your team, you are ready to get down to the nitty gritty of identifying what specifically you want to achieve in your advocacy efforts. You need to remember that advocacy is a process that will probably go on for a long time. Advocacy is not a single meeting or meetings where you present your demands or expectations. Advocacy is really a series of steps that need to be considered. So, here are some questions you may want to discuss with your support person or family members before sitting down with your child's educational team:

1. What is the purpose of your efforts?

2. What is the specific goal(s) you want to achieve?

3. What are you ultimately hoping to accomplish?

4. What are acceptable and unacceptable outcomes?

Remember to be specific when answering these questions. For example, if one of your concerns is that your child is not learning to read and is below grade-level, your goal might be that you "want your child to be able to read." This isn't specific enough. A better goal would be to "identify and implement a reading program specific for children with reading disabilities, with identifiable benchmarks for measuring achievement." After you have your goal(s), you can work with your team to develop a plan and strategies for reaching that goal. It's in this step that you may want to share facts or evidence to support a specific program for your child and how the school's available resources can be used to put the plan in place.

Limited human and financial resources may be a barrier to putting your plan in place, so what is reasonable on one side of the table may not be realistic for the other side of the table. Keeping emotions in check is essential when wrangling with difficult decisions. Always remain calm and rational, and avoid making any comments or discussions personal. This type of approach will help you maintain effective relationships and teams with others who are in decision-making positions for your child. All your advocacy efforts should be dedicated to helping your child experience success, happiness, and confidence.

Taking Care of Yourself

Finally, advocacy is tough duty! While taking care of your child, take care of yourself. No matter what, you have to remember to do things that make you and other family members feel good, happy, and stress-free. Siblings and extended family members can feel the stress and frustration of the advocacy process. Try to look at the process from the 35,000-foot level. This can help you maintain a balance so you take care of you while advocating for your child, as well as taking care of your other family members. Here are some suggestions:

- Work fun and recreation into your schedule
- Keep your loving family relationships healthy and stable
- Listen to music
- Dance
- Go out for a meal
- Enjoy nature
- Have a family game night
- Schedule date nights (and don't talk about your kids)
- Watch a movie

- Meditate
- Exercise

Whatever it is that brings you happiness, renewal, or relaxation, make it part of your plan. You can't be effective for your child if you are exhausted and unhappy. You need to feel happiness, joy, and confidence just as much as your children do!

Reflections

1. Who would be a good support person(s) and why?

2. Who do I need to build relationships with to help my child? What do I need to do to build and keep those relationships?

3. Who should be part of my child's team?

4. What am I advocating for and why?

5. What do I need to do to take care of myself?

8

From Isolation to Building Teams for Your Child and Yourself

Since her son, eight-year-old Anthony, was born, Ericka knew that her child was different. He seemed to be upset by loud sounds, and didn't like to eat certain textures. As a kindergartener, Anthony became upset when his sister won a Martial Arts contest, was awarded a special trophy, and honored at school. Anthony couldn't seem to control his emotions. He would blow up easily. Many times, he'd refuse to get out of bed to get ready for school. No matter what he did, he just didn't seem to fit in. He had a difficult time making friends and keeping friends. He had difficulty writing and reading. He just couldn't seem to focus in class, and appeared to be wandering in his own thoughts.

So, it was quite a surprise that when Anthony was in third grade and tested by an outside psychologist, the report came back that in addition to his attention deficit hyperactive disorder, fine motor skills difficulty, reading problems, and low self-esteem, he was also gifted! These test results made no sense to both Ericka and her husband. How could their son show such difficulty with reading and handwriting, getting along with other children—including his own sister—making friends, and be gifted at the same time?

They had visited so many different professionals who claimed they could help their son, only to leave town. Others had "started off strongly," only to lack follow through, bringing Ericka and her husband back to square one.

But now, Ericka and her husband had an outside professional who saw their son's true potential. They had someone they could speak to who understood their son and gave them hope. They experienced their own confidence-building as they met with the therapist to make a plan for their son's therapy. They met with other professionals, coaches, and community leaders as they integrated Anthony into focused activities where he had opportunities for success. Ericka and her husband realized they could achieve more when others were on their side. They could focus on their son's abilities, in addition to his disabilities. They decided to let go of the shame, guilt, negative feelings, and harmful thoughts. The therapist gave them the courage they needed to move forward. Together, confidently, they began to build their team!

What's a Parent to Do? It's not Easy to Walk the Path Alone

When you have a child who is different, you find yourself searching for answers to so many questions, like "Why doesn't my child..."

- Eat crunchy foods?
- Share with his friend every day, instead of sharing one day and hoarding everything the next?
- Wear clothes that have tags?
- Bend his knees and jump?

- Hold a pencil?
- Understand what I say?

The list can go on and on, as you wonder why your child does the things he does and why he doesn't do other things like other children his age.

You go through a process of searching for anyone who can give you advice and help your child. You search for answers, looking for other parents you can speak with, searching the Internet, reading books, going to meetings—all in the effort of reaching the goal for your child's success.

In Ericka's situation, after all the years of searching for answers from professionals, from kindergarten to first grade, second grade, and into third grade, she was not given answers. Anthony was not "bad enough" to receive an individual education program (IEP). He was in "regular" classrooms with "regular" children; however, he didn't seem "regular" with issues surrounding his difficulty reading, paying attention, writing, and making friends. As a mother, Ericka carried feelings of hurt and shame—of not belonging and being on the outside looking in—as did Anthony.

Seven Isolating Solutions

You search for solutions, but find more isolation. For example:

1) *Seeking answers from professionals who do not care.*

   You sought out professionals, with well-known reputations. who were ill-equipped to handle the many different facets of your child's skills and behavior. They didn't listen to you sincerely.

2) *Getting to know parents of children without differences.*

   You may have spent many weeks getting close to other parents of children your child's age who don't have learning differences. Meeting those parents and learning about their families made you feel more disconnected and lonely.

3) *Setting up playdates.*

Many times, these play groups turned upside down. Your child became upset when another child won a game, or he tried to catch a ball, fell down, and was laughed at.

4) *Introducing your child to other children.*

Your child may continue to feel "less than enough," "left out," and "more different" meeting other children. "You two kids can be such good friends," you say. Your child withdraws, not knowing what a "good friend" is, what a good friend talks about and shares, or how to take another person's perspective or engage in back and forth conversation. So, the introduction flops.

5) *Surfing the Internet and/or viewing YouTube videos, or Ted Talks.*

As a parent, you want to understand your child. So, you surf the Internet, put in key words (i.e., sensory processing disorder, Attention Deficit Hyperactive Disorder, etc.). Looking at the screen, you realize you are still alone, with no one to speak with, and no external physical comfort or support.

6) *Reading books, magazines, journal articles.*

Looking for more answers, you read to gain insights about your child. Again, you are reading alone. Finding people who are interested in hearing about the book and your child may not be readily available.

7) *Going to meetings.*

> When you go to meetings, you can learn new information, discover new theories and strategies, and gain greater understanding about your child. When the meeting is over, you are on your own again. You might meet someone new and exchange contact information, only to never hear from them again.

After trying many of the above strategies, you certainly have more information—but you are still isolated. You are still alone. So, what's a parent to do? It is difficult when your child feels alone and isolated, but it's even more difficult to be a parent and feel alone and isolated too!

Building a Stellar First-Class Team

What is a team? "A team is a group of individuals working together to achieve a common goal."

Working together allows each member to:

- Feel more powerful in numbers
- Complement, commit, and collaborate in a coordinated fashion
- Contribute their skills and talents into a synergistic whole
- Move forward and reach desired goals that build your child's confidence, joy, and success

Team members should:

- Be dependable and reliable
- Care about your child's well-being
- Be sustainable and predictable
- Want to see your child succeed and live a confident and joyful life

Who Will Lead the Team?

You will! You're the best person to be Captain of the Team! You know your child best!

You know:

- Your child's specific behaviors
- What makes your child happy or sad
- The challenges and struggles your child faces daily
- Your child's triumphs
- Your child's goals

You have personal relationships that allow you to invite others to join your team. They will be more willing to join the team when asked by someone they know.

Who Will be Your Team Members?

Your team can consist of family, friends, professionals, counselors or coaches, members of the academic school community, health community, and social and extra-curricular activities communities.

If your concerns are mostly about educational needs of your child, you may want to build an educational team consisting of yourself, possibly a special education teacher (if there is one), the principal, a tutor, a regular teacher, a school psychologist, and other therapists and specialists.

If your child has health issues, you may want to build a health team including yourself, a nurse, a physician, other specialists who are working with your child's health needs, therapists, and teachers.

If you have identified family needs, you may want to build a family support team consisting of yourself, specific members of your family, a religious counselor or leader, therapist, social worker, family physician, or family advocate.

You may have a team of a variety of members with whom you feel comfortable, and whose judgment you trust. Sometimes you can look "outside the box" to find people who would make good team members and have your child's interests at heart. For example, many working women have shared that if it weren't for their bosses, they'd not be able to keep their child's medical appointments, therapy appointments, or school meetings. Inviting your boss to be part of a team can show your boss you think highly of him or her.

Teambuilding 101

As a team, you must determine how your group will run smoothly and efficiently to accomplish its goals.

8 questions to ask yourself:

- Who would I like to invite to join my child's team?
- How will I invite them? (personally, via e-mail, in a letter, etc.)
- How will I keep in contact with the members? (by phone, face-to-face meetings, email)
- How will the members keep in contact with one another?
- How frequently will we meet? (every month, every two months, whenever needed)
- How will decisions be made? (Will the Captain listen to input and make ultimate decisions, or will there be consensus?)
- When will new members be added?
- Will there be a maximum number of team members?

Teams can help:

- Focus on the ultimate direction needed for your child's success
- Bring together talents and expertise in its members who can answer questions and guide you
- Create a space where you do not feel alone
- Lift you up when you are down
- Build your own confidence in what you are doing
- Help you see the humor in everyday events, even if you don't see it
- Support you while making a difference for your child
- Further your own growth
- Celebrate your child's successes
- Celebrate your successes, too!

Building Your Team One Step at a Time

At first, you may be at a loss of what to do. But once you start talking with other parents, coming from passion and commitment, you'll realize that you *can* build a team for your child.

Right now, you may not be sure who would join your team. Begin searching for anyone who could give you advice and help your child. You can search out professionals already working with your child. You may also search out family members and friends.

You may feel that it's as if you're a door to door salesperson, "dragging your child with you." You may never have thought that building a team was possible. You may never have thought that building a first-class team could provide valuable services for your child in his areas of need (e.g., focusing, academics, social skills, acceptance, support, and raising self-esteem could become a reality). It is all possible!

Let Your Child Build His Own Team

With an older child, you may find that your child wants to be involved in choosing his own team. Maybe he wants to include his grandmother or favorite uncle. Maybe it's his favorite therapist or his coach. It could also be his good old dog. Giving your child the opportunity to choose members of his team will provide the "buy in" needed to build confidence, joy, and ultimate success!

Never Give Up

It is easy to give up. Someone turns down your invitation to join your team. Someone cannot commit with their own schedule. When Ericka was asked what turned the corner for her, she said it was her own grit of never giving up.

When she became "The Captain of the Amazing Anthony Team," she...

- became active in her son's school as a member of the parent teacher association.
- volunteered in her son's class.
- learned about her son's strengths and needs.
- became open to meet families of other children who were *different.* She no longer had the vision to make Anthony like the other children in his classroom. She now had the option to find other children like Anthony, and relate to other mothers who were going through the same thing she was—and invite them to her team.
- met friends and professionals in the community and her son's school, to find a group who could offer guidance and support—not just to her son, but to her and her husband and family as well.

Building a stellar first-class team doesn't come easily. Here are some steps you can take:

- Ask for names of professionals from other parents of children who are considered "different."
- Seek out parents who might serve on your team who know more than you do.
- Have playdates with other moms of children who are a bit "different."
- Strengthen yourself as you assemble more and more professionals who can serve your child.

What's a Captain to Do?

As the Captain, you'll be the one who brings together the therapists, educators, family, and friends. You'll get the team members to talk together, e-mail one another, and be on the "same page." You'll keep the group together for the common goal. You'll decide how often you want to hold a meeting with your stellar team to keep focused on what is best for your child and receive the support you need.

Also, as Captain, know your child's educational rights. Learn as much as you can about federal, state, and local laws, codes, and regulations.

Knowledge is a Blessing

Each member of the team brings different knowledge to the group. Having a varied group of team members is a blessing.

If you have people in the academic world on your team, they can advise you about what to expect from early intervention programs—preschool to elementary school, middle school, high school, vocational school, and/or college. They will know the meaning of acronyms "thrown around" during meetings. They also know more about available educational services that can be provided to your child for greater success, increasing your child's self-esteem.

Having people from the medical community on your team (i.e., a doctor, nurse, or healthcare professional) can assist you through the system of care and best choices of programs for your child. They may know more about your health insurance plan and what services are covered for your child. For example, some insurance plans will pay for applied behavioral analysis in your home with a diagnosis of autism. Some insurance companies will pay for speech and language therapy if medical necessity can be proven.

Therapists on your team can assist in knowing about programs and best practices, and available resources in the community. They can help identify terms used by professionals at meetings and/or during assessments.

In Ericka's case, her "Amazing Anthony Team" consisted of her son's occupational therapist, school psychologist, outside psychologist, classroom teacher, the principal, family physician, her husband, herself, and a family friend!

As your team unfolds, you will gain confidence. You will become more optimistic in your child's future. Ericka became optimistic about Anthony's future, something she had not felt before.

Building a Team of Support Just for You

As your child's team works smoothly, you realize he has a wonderful group focusing on his needs to lead to his success. However, you soon recognize that you don't have one for yourself. Your significant other may be "buried in work," but it is you who is feeling buried. You never get your child off your mind. You wonder how he's doing in school. Is he happy, sad, being bullied? Is his teacher being compassionate, or pointing him out for not following the class rules? Is he being kept inside during recess because he has not finished his written work, again? Have other children invited him to play, or is he being made fun of because he can't kick the soccer ball?

As a parent, you want to praise and offer accolades to your child. Yet sometimes, you may just want to scream! How can you get up day after day, never knowing what mood your child will be in when waking up? Will your child be loving, angry, or will he kick you out of his room? Will he yell at you because you don't know what he really needs? Will he refuse to get out of bed until *you* actually put on his school clothes and act as funny as you can, to have him laugh and see how silly getting ready for school can be?

When you find yourself no longer being able to pretend that your child is like any other child his age, and begin to admit to yourself and others that your loving child also has some differences that make it harder to accomplish schoolwork (even if gifted), it may be time to find your own support team. This team is to support your own emotional needs.

Reaching Out to Others

You may seek out professionals to see if they know of existing mom's or dad's groups, or know of moms or dads who would like to form a group. You may find a support group from your religious affiliation or a group run by a therapist.

By reaching out to others, you can find some peace knowing that you are not alone. In your own personal team, you may cry about your child's trials and tribulations, and other mothers or fathers will fully understand your plight. You can talk about how it took three years for someone to listen to you at the school district level, and other team moms who experienced the same treatment will offer support. You can talk about how your marriage is sometimes on the edge because you and your husband see your son's behavior differently.

Others may be walking the same path you are. By being together, you can climb the mountain! Finding a support team for yourself can make all the difference in the world toward feeling sane, staying married, and being joyful with your own abilities to parent a child with differences.

Reflections

1. Are you willing to be the Captain of your child's team, and bring together all the professionals and others who serve your child to form a first-class team?

2. Will you be able to allow your older child to participate in choosing team members of his or her own team, based on his or her interests?

3. Will you be able to keep on going, and not give up? If yes, how will you do that even if there is no end in sight?

4. Are you willing to get out of your comfort zone and seek out other parents of children who are different to form a mom's support team for yourself, or join one that is already in existence?

5. Will you be able to see humor in everyday occurrences, and continue to move ahead to help your child reach his goals?

9

Creating Communities of Confidence and Joy

Hannah is in the fifth grade and is quiet and shy. She has struggled with learning, though she isn't formally enrolled in special education. She doesn't have an IEP, but has had a student study team in the past. Though Hannah has learning challenges, she is gifted and talented with dance and movement. She is aware that learning is difficult for her. She knows that she needs extra help from her teacher when other students don't need any help at all. She knows that it takes her lots more time to complete assignments than the others, and she often has lots of extra homework because she can't get her work done in class. Hannah tries to "fit in" with her classmates, but just doesn't. She has a few friends, but not ones that she hangs out with on weekends or holidays.

Her parents are concerned about her lack of friends as much as they are about her learning. At home, Hannah is sad, quiet, and withdrawn, which concerns her parents. They've decided that they need to be proactive and get Hannah involved in programs and activities that will allow her to grow and thrive—and activities that will let her talents and gifts be recognized and celebrated. They realize that she needs a community beyond what her family and classroom can offer. They investigate several potential programs and organizations that they think will bring happiness and confidence to their bright daughter. They enroll Hannah in a local dance company—a summer resident dance camp—and an acting class. Her parents find stable, safe, and healthy communities for Hannah and watch their shy and quiet daughter become the happy, confident, and outgoing person they knew she could be.

What Does 'Community' Mean?

When you hear such things as "educational community," "medical community," "sports community," or "art community," you know exactly who or what is being discussed. Our entire social structure is built on community, as well as the history of the world. No one person has ever altered the pages of history solely by the efforts of him/herself, without some kind a support group or community. Martin Luther King, Jr. could not have taken on the civil rights movement without the men and women who stood by him. Maya Angelou did not make literary history by herself. No artist gains fame and recognition without support from others. No athlete wins medals or trophies without coaches, fans, or trainers. Frankly, few businesses can stay relevant without collaboration and support. *Community* can't happen without collaboration, and community, in a social sense, is necessary for creating a sense of belonging in all of us.

Community means more than a body of people who live or work in the same place. Community in terms of *confidence and joy communities* means something more powerful: joint ownership and joint commitment. That means everyone shares in making confidence and joy happen, and it's a priority. It means that everyone is invested in it and everyone has a piece of the pie. What a fabulous concept: everyone committed to building and sustaining confidence and joy in a child! We have to remember that everyone is better together than alone, and what better cause is there than ensuring a child's sense of confidence and joy? Creating these types of communities for kids with learning differences can shape the outcome of children's lives. But how does that happen?

Well, since parents are the first external support system for their children, the task of building communities of support becomes their job. Practically speaking, confidence and joy communities don't formally exist and won't happen on their own; they have to be created by the parents of the learning different child.

8 Joy and Confidence Communities at Your Fingertips

We are not referring to communities with homes, trees, parks, and shopping areas. We are referring to *groups of people with shared interests and passions.* These communities are going to be intentional and not contrived in their purpose, composition, and interests. A lot of thought goes into creating a *community.* Parents will ask themselves, *What groups, activities, or situations that my child is or will be involved in will be environments that can support my child's confidence and joy?* This question starts the process of being intentional in building this particular type of community. Good, solid communities are sustainable. They are safe and open places where a menagerie of different, bright, and talented children—as well as adults—can come together and share their skills, talents, ideas, and gifts without fear of being judged, rejected, teased, or bullied.

So, what are some common potential communities?

- **Play groups**: Many younger children belong to play groups, where like-minded parents bring their children to spend time together playing. These groups allow all children to learn from each other by interacting, imitating, and experimenting. Parents can seek out specific play groups or form one of their own. Letting other parents know that you are on a mission to intentionally build confidence and joy as a part of your child's development will get that "joint ownership"; and it will not only benefit your child, but all the children in the group.

- **Daycare**: Working families rely on daycare while they are busy working. Daycare is a valuable support system for your child. A daycare setting provides an environment, activities, and relationships for a child that can build confidence and joy consistently. Discuss thoughtful and intentional ways that your daycare setting can be a community of support for your child's confidence and joy.

- **Clubs**: Belonging to clubs and organizations is a part of being a kid. Selecting a club or organization that is a "good fit" for your child is essential for building confidence and joy. Select a club or organization that matches your child's talents, interests, gifts, and natural abilities. Select one that your child will enjoy and experience a sense of accomplishment through learning new things, building new relationships, and, most importantly, building confidence. Let the leader know the specifics about your child's learning differences and how they may impact his/her participation in the club or organization. Set up a system for communicating with the leader, and work on implementing specific instructional and learning strategies that will be useful in making the experience fun and successful.

- **Sports**: Organized team, recreational, and club sports are very popular with children. These sporting opportunities attract children of all levels of talent, experience, and mastery. Children with learning challenges may be athletically gifted or talented, but have difficulty succeeding because they have attentional issues, trouble understanding and following instructions, difficulty remembering what they have been told, or just "don't get it." Parents really have to be thoughtful and intentional in helping their child select a sport that matches his gifts, talents, abilities, learning style, and limitations—as well as temperament. Participating in sports gives a child the opportunity to develop new physical and cognitive skills, develop new relationships, master challenges, set and achieve goals (large or small), and learn about winning and losing. Sports can be a perfect community of support for any child, but especially children with learning challenges. Once parents have identified and selected "the" sport for their child, then their child's confidence and joy can thrive because the community is a safe and open place where all the children come together to have fun, share their talents and skills, and make and keep friends.

- **Music and art programs**: Like sports, this is another example of a community of support for children. Music, painting, singing, dance, theater, woodworking, drawing, writing, photography, and crafting are programs that let kids learn about their creative gifts and talents. Like other communities that are created to support the development of a child's confidence and joy, participation in ongoing and structured music and art programs can build a sense of accomplishment, achievement, mastery, happiness, and fulfillment. All children want and need to be awesome at something—to be a star. There is nothing better than being "the best" at something to build confidence and joy in a child, especially a child with challenges in the classroom.

  Parents can be creative in building this type of community for your child. You can host get-togethers for families who share the same interests, encourage your child to enter community contests, encourage your child to take his/ her talent to other community events, enroll your child in summer camps for music, arts, science, or technology to support these interests, encourage your child to be a peer mentor, or even start a small club for a particular area of interest. Sometimes, parents have to be creative in finding what their child can excel in—but whatever it may be, let them be a star!

- **Church programs or activities:** Youth programs at a church, synagogue, or mosque are excellent communities for children to experience confidence and joy. These programs are geared toward engaging likeminded children in activities that are fun, interactive, and often creative and offered in safe environments. If these types of programs aren't interesting to you and your child, that isn't a problem. There are so many other communities available to your child. If you already are members of a church, synagogue, or mosque, you may want to really check out the children's programs to be certain that they're a "good fit" for your child and his/her needs. Talking with the teacher(s) would be a good first step so you can share information about your child and what you are seeking. You might be considering a program for the first time. If so, take the time to "visit" several programs before you make a decision. Not all children's programs are equal, so like every other decision you make about your child, be sure that this is with purpose and intention. Any community that your child participates in has to be one that will build and keep confidence and joy a priority. With confidence and joy, anything is possible!

- **Camps:** Day camps, residence camps, nature camps, science camps, technology camps, sports camps, and club camps are wonderful community experiences for all children. Though these camps are typically seasonal and temporary, they offer children opportunities as well as programs that can build their confidence and bring them joy. These camp communities also offer opportunities and experiences for children to grow and push themselves, because they don't have parents or other family members stepping in and helping when they run into problems or face challenges. The camp community experience can be just awesome! Children become part of a community where they have to engage with others, make new friends, be flexible and adaptable, learn new skills, participate in new activities, and often step out of their comfort zone. Talk about confidence building! Most camp counselors are extraordinarily skilled in working with children, and their enthusiasm for what they are doing is almost magical in getting children to be comfortable with the entire camp experience—especially with participating in and doing things for the first time. For most children, a camp experience can be a huge confidence builder. When children return home from camp, they are typically excited and happy about all the wonderful new things that they learned, experienced, and did. It's a great opportunity for confidence and joy! So, check with the community resources in your area to find a camp that would be appropriate for your child and works within your family's framework.

- **Schools:** Schools really are their own community. The nice thing about the school community is that it is typically a predictable environment, and the schedule and activities provide consistency and continuity. Children with learning differences do best when they have structure and familiarity. Another benefit of a school community is that, for the child with learning differences, there is often a "team" of educational professionals in place to provide the necessary resources to make learning more successful for your child. As parents, your job is to be sure that the school community is one where your child can learn, grow, and thrive despite having learning challenges. The school community is one that can have the most powerful effect on your child's confidence and joy. Whether it is during a parent-teacher conference, a student study team, or an IEP, all educational professionals need to know that your child's confidence and joy are as important as his/her academic and social achievement and success.

A final thought about community: community is tangible, cohesive, and brings kids together in ways that allow them to do things they could not have done alone. The right choice of communities for your child can be empowering in ways that other passive types of activities are. Remember that being in community is active and not passive. Everyone is working together, but everyone is working and participating. Active participation means doing, doing means accomplishing, accomplishing means success, success means confidence, and confidence brings happiness and joy.

10 Strategies to Get Your Child Involved in a Community

Finding a community to build your child's confidence and joy isn't all that different from advocating for your child. It's really a form of advocacy. You are basically letting others know that you want your child to be a part of a group of like-minded kids who want to learn, grow, and thrive in a safe and fun environment. You want your child to be actively involved in shared activities, programs, or events that can build his/her confidence and joy. You can do this!

But how do you get started? Here are a few suggestions:

1. Know what your child needs and what makes him/her happy and feeling confident. Knowing this can help you to choose from the many *communities* that are available. Is your child at his/her best when outdoors, in sports, with animals, and so forth?

2. Talk to other parents. Ask them about activities or programs that their children are involved in and learn the structure, purpose, and value of these programs. Ask what works and doesn't work, and why they selected that particular *community* for their child.

3. Talk to your child's teacher and educational team. Get their input on what type of program would be best for your child. Be specific in what you want for your child and that your overall desire is to build your child's joy and confidence.

4. Access community calendars and guides in learning the various options available that match your child's interests and talents.

5. When making a selection, be sure that the program's schedule works well with your family schedule. Otherwise, your child's participation can become a burden.

6. Consider your family resources: time, energy, money, and people. Do you have enough time for active participation? Do you have the energy to make your child's participation fun and successful for him/her? What are the short- and long-term costs, and how will these costs impact your family's budget? Finally, who will provide the transportation, physical support, and other "things" that will certainly need to be addressed? These considerations are essential to the success and happiness that comes with being in a community.

7. Check them out! Go first without your child to see what you think about this program being a good *community* for your child. Talk with other parents whose children are involved. Talk with the adult leader. Ask questions! Get as much information as possible by observing, collaborating, and "investigating." After you have done all of this, go again and take your child to check it out. Children have completely different perspectives than parents. Together, you can select the right community for your child.

8. By the way, your child doesn't need to know that your selection of a community is for building his/her confidence and joy. You may want to ask your child which program they think will help them grow and learn, make more friends, and make them happy. Keep it simple.

9. You may select one community or, depending on the type, you may have more than one. Whatever you decide, stay committed. Give it time. Anything new may be uncomfortable at first. Don't quit and don't jump to other communities too soon. Let your child experience meeting new friends, trying new activities, learning new skills, and achieving success. This will make your child both happy and confident.

10. Celebrate! Celebrate your successful mission of finding a community where your child can grow and thrive outside the family unit. Celebrate the new opportunities your child will experience with new adult models and new friends.

Celebrate your child's achievements and success. Really celebrate your child's joy and confidence.

Communities of support are really just support systems—but in this case, not just an ordinary support system. These are communities that support building and keeping confidence and joy in the hearts of children with learning challenges. Keeping confidence and joy alive in children is essential to their adult lives. Everyone is in this together, committing to children's confidence and joy to create a better world for all of us.

Reflections

1. What does community mean to me? To my child?

2. What constitutes a "good community" for my child?

3. What are some potential "communities" that would help my child grow and thrive?

4. What are some possible communities that will build and keep joy and confidence in my child's heart?

5. What are three things I can do now to get started on getting my child involved in a community of support? When do I start and when will he/she begin?

10

All Children Want to Succeed: Smart in Their Own Way

Lia remembers Carson had asthma, and was always sick with something—including ear infections. He was a late talker. At five years of age, his tonsils and adenoids were removed. Carson would only wear soft clothes and silk underwear. His room had to be pitch black, and he wore a mask over his face to sleep. His bed had to be put in the corner instead of in the middle of his room. When his bed was in the corner, he felt more secure and he'd be out of the sunlight. He couldn't stand it when the sun crept through the window into his eyes.

Lia knew something was different about her son. At three years of age, he would ask her, "What's your name?" Lia told Carson, "Mommy." Carson repeated out loud, "Mommy" three times in a row. "Mommy," "Mommy," "Mommy,"—then he closed his eyes as if trying to hold the memory of his mother's name in his brain. But when the next day came, he would ask again, "What's your name?" He couldn't remember the word "Mommy."

As a parent and professional, Lia had raised another child and was also a schoolteacher once recognized as teacher of the year in her home state of New Jersey. She knew when her son couldn't remember "Mommy" that something was different about Carson. She took him to see a specialist, several specialists, and they told her, "He's fine. Sometimes people don't remember names." Lia said, "But Mommy? When have you heard of a child not remembering the word 'Mommy?'"

Carson also showed difficulty recognizing letters, reading, and writing. So again, Lia had Carson tested in first grade, and again the "experts" blew her off—even though she saw and knew in her heart that Carson had difficulty with auditory processing, auditory memory, attention, and speech.

Finally, the school gave him one year of resource writing—but they didn't officially classify him as a child with special needs, so they wouldn't give him services. It wasn't until the fourth grade that the school Carson attended gave him speech therapy services. Carson discovered his passion in middle school. That was the day his economics teacher challenged the class to use pretend money (each child got the same amount) and buy stocks. At the end of the semester, the person with the most pretend money would be declared the winner! Carson was up to the challenge.

He loved the money game. It encouraged him to read The Wall Street Journal and Money Magazine. He used his intellect to think about which stocks would be good ones, to buy and sell at the best times, and make a profit. After weeks of wheeling and dealing, Carson was the winner! His love for money paid off. Something that he was a natural with, and felt so confident with, was something that his other classmates could not tackle.

Carson was different. He was also smart!

Different and Smart Can Live Together

Just because your child is different does not mean that your child is lacking intelligence or the ability to learn. Your child with a learning difference may have gifts and talents, unique unto himself. Having a learning difference means just that... you have a learning difference.

A child with a memory processing disorder, speech and language problems, spelling difficulties, or ADHD (like Anthony in Chapter 8) can succeed. They may not be able to write, but they can build a magnificent architectural structure. They may not be able to read, but they can problem-solve a mathematical problem. They may be bothered by emotional outbursts when deregulated, but they can sing like an angel.

Children on the spectrum may have heightened skills that make them superior in intelligence to other children. A child with a speech and language delay may have a high intellect, just not be able to speak and be understood. Their receptive language skills may be superior; it is just the expressive part that is not functional. Any child who is different in one way can be bright in another.

All the children whose stories have been shared in this book have succeeded. Some of the children have matured into adulthood and had children of their own. They are successful contributors to society, and are giving back to the communities that supported them.

Finding the Sparkle in Your Children's Eyes, the Passion in Their Hearts

Carson, like all children with differences, wanted to succeed—and he did! Lia found the sparkle in her son's eyes that ignited his desire to get up each morning and go to school. For Carson, it was money! In first grade, he would cut and paste two sheets of paper together, and make them into a bookmark. When his parents' friends came to his house, he would sell each bookmark for one dollar. His aunt would also give him nickel paper rolls. He would spend an hour, or more, wrapping them to bring to the bank for five dollars. (His older brother made high grades easily, and wanted no part of the money that Carson loved.)

Every child has skills and talents. Sometimes these skills emerge and are visible, and other times the skills and interests need to be uncovered. Parents must face the challenges and find ways they can uncover their child's skills. They must discover what motivates their child to get up each morning and do their best.

As the parent of a child with a difference or many differences, you must continue to be your child's advocate and the Team Captain for your child. You must never give up. Children with differences, like Carson, may not qualify for special education. Lia had Carson tutored at his house until he was in middle school to improve his writing and language skills. He would study, all week, for the spelling words for his Friday test, and he would get four words correct and couldn't remember the rest of the spelling list.

Yet Lia found the sparkle in her son's eyes. She discovered what made her child "tick." As mentioned previously, for Carson, it was money. Now, however, when he was in middle school, Carson found his passion for stocks. When he "bought" Microsystems, and his money increased he was sold. Carson's dad saw how Carson was succeeding in his ability to make money, so Carson's dad bought the real Microsystems stock for Carson. Carson started following the stock market, and learned more and more about it. The boy who could not read or remember the word "Mommy" was now reading *Money Magazine* and *The Wall Street Journal*. He won the stock market challenge in his class and never looked back.

Being Smart Requires 'Knowing'

Children with learning differences may need to discover what tools they can use to help reveal their talents, gain confidence and joyfulness, and succeed. For example, having a 504 plan that Carson's mother procured for him allowed Carson to take standardized tests independently, and for extended time periods. When he sat for the Scholastic Achievement Test for college entry, he used his 504 plan accommodations. He took the standardized test in a quiet room, away from other students, with additional time allowance. He had someone read the questions aloud for him, too.

Carson was able to focus on the test with reduced anxiety. He was accepted into eleven out of the twelve colleges for which he applied. Smart? Yes! Distinctive? Yes! Genius? In his own way!

For a child with learning differences, achieving success from being smart takes a certain amount of "knowing":

- *Knowing* what your passion is
- *Knowing* what your talents and gifts are and what you excel in
- *Knowing* how you study most efficiently
- *Knowing* how you perform your best
- *Knowing* ways to focus
- *Knowing* ways to reduce anxiety and nervousness
- *Knowing* ways to make friends
- *Knowing* how to "stick with it"

Carson went on to college by choosing a College Park Scholars program consisting of a separate dormitory at the University of Maryland. In this program, students had their own dormitory and the studies were broken up into ten subcategories (i.e., science, business, etc.). Carson went to classes in the dorm so he was in a smaller group. This made a big school smaller for him—and easier for him to function. Carson then went on to an Ivy League University for his Master's degree. He continued to shine.

By knowing your child's own strengths, unique talents and gifts, and which way of learning works best, achievement and success are attainable.

Encouraging Success

Parents might wonder what will become of their children. Will they succeed? Will they find happiness? Will they find a significant other? Will they have children of their own? Will their family be loving?

Carson didn't think he would do well in college, but he did. His friends would go out and leave him in his room studying. When they came back, he was still studying. His determination to succeed came from within. He was smart. He worked hard and was determined to succeed, just like the other children whose stories we have shared.

Carson loved what he did. He wasn't afraid to work hard. He focused on something he loved, and hard work translated into success. At twenty-five years of age, in addition to the apartment he lived in, he bought a beach house. Today, he is happily married and a dad. He lives in a multi-million-dollar home in a prestigious neighborhood, on over an acre of land. He has already bought a small business that supports children with differences and allows him to give back to his community. He plans to retire when he is forty and then take over the daily operations of the business. Do you think children with learning differences are smart? You bet they are!

Strategies to Improve Brain Functioning

In addition to parents being detectives, advocates, cheerleaders, best fans, and Team Captains, they are discovering ways they can promote relaxation and reduce tension and anxiety in their children. By using these easy strategies, brain function improves, hormones release, and intellectual functioning improves. Various strategies include breathing, affirmations, mindfulness, music, laughter, yoga, music, and touch. Children can reduce negativity, anxiety, and doubt, and improve their confidence, happiness, and brain functioning.

More and more children with learning differences and special needs are experiencing these neuroscientific approaches to reduce anxiety, promote well-being, and excel.

Passion Detective 101

We know that children with learning differences are smart. But sometimes, it takes a village to uncover your child's talents and gifts. Whether it is literature, math, writing, the stock market, art, music, medicine, technology, fixing cars, being kind, or teaching, when your child finds the spark within—or you discover the spark—it will be easier to stick to the necessary tasks needed to succeed.

Besides being the learning style detective discussed in Chapter 1, you can now become the *passion detective.* See what gets your child's attention, and use the 6 E's to provide opportunities for building confidence, joy and success:

- Expose your child's style of learning (what is your child's learning style?)
- Explore opportunities for success
- Encourage activities your child appears to be passionate about
- Enrich your child's experiences

- Excel your child's success by incorporating the way he learns best into any activity
- Enjoy these moments

Sam saw his son, Miles, jump off his chaise lounge at a hotel pool to run across to a man who was holding an owl. Miles pet the owl, asked the man questions about the owl's age, name, and size. Seeing Miles' behavior startled his father. Sam never knew his son was so interested in wildlife and animals. Sam decided to take his son to the wildlife park and explore the animal habitats. Miles began learning more about animal habitats and enthusiastically shared this information with his class, to the delight of his teacher and classmates.

Let Your Child's Brightness Shine

Here are *five easy tips* to allow your child's brightness to shine:

1) *Don't compare* your child to another child. Your child is smart in his own way. Celebrate the differences and love each child unconditionally. For example, Carson's brother Jeremy could speak and read two languages at the age of four. He also did not care about money, and would never roll up nickels and keep the money. He'd rather not have the money if he had to roll it up! Carson grew up and became a successful Commodities Broker. His brother, Jeremy, grew up and became a successful doctor!

2) *Build the foundation* for greater success by using current neuroscience brainwork activities that allow your child to regulate his emotions and become focused, mindful, and in a quiet alert state where learning takes place more readily.

3) *Allow your child* to engage in activities other than academics. It might be swimming or Tai Kwon Do that he enjoys and excels in. Extracurricular activities play a great part in balancing out your child, so thinking about academics and school subjects are not always on his mind.

4) *Let your child lead and show you* what he enjoys doing. Don't always put rules on your child's activities that thwart him from showing you what he can do, and what he enjoys doing.

5) *Participate in your child's accomplishments and successes*, encouraging more success. Seeing a parent at a game or recital enriches the loving memories and provides joyful support for your child, who knows that you care. If you cannot attend an event, find other ways of showing your interest—a little note in your child's lunchbox, a handwritten card you can mail to your child, or a quick FaceTime call.

Your *child will not be a child forever*. Do not be afraid of going the extra mile to find out what your child needs to succeed. Your child's success is truly their desire. Having your child reach his goals leads to confidence and joy, success, and well-being— socially, emotionally, and personally. All children want to be successful.

Growing Success, Confidence, and Joy for Your *Child*

Your child is like a seed wanting to bloom, with unique talents, skills, and a beauty all his or her own. With the right ingredients, he or she will grow and blossom. The seed holds all the potential. What are you doing to help your child's seed germinate into a flower? How are you nurturing the soil? How are you positioning your flower for growth? Like a seed you've planted, it requires water and sunlight and nourishment to grow. You are the gardener in your child's life.

As parents or educators, our job is to nurture our children and help them become the best they can be, to reach their full potential. Like a flower, children are part of the garden of life, and each child contributes to the magnificence of our world. We are all in this together. Together, we learn and grow. Unique talents delight the landscape. Feeling successful, your child's confidence and joy can soar, reaching toward the sky.

10 Easy Ways to Bring Out 'Smart-ness' When There is a Learning Difference

1. Get support for your child when you notice differences

2. Seek outside assistance if your child's school will not offer assistance

3. Become your child's advocate

4. Find out your child's likes and interests

5. Use those interests to encourage success

6. Develop a home program, as needed

7. Encourage friendships that support your child's likes and interests

8. Continue to use your team to keep the progress going

9. Find ways to support your child through methods of mindfulness, affirmations, breathing, healthy diet, positive thoughts, proper sleep, movement, music, and laughter

10. Remember to have fun and experience the humor in life, together

Every child has a special talent or gift. Every child wants to succeed. We have shown you a variety of children with differences. We have shared their stories, their challenges, and their victories. We have shared their families' struggles and triumphs, too.

The road to confidence, joy, and success begins with you. We hope that the course we have set out for you—along with the tips, strategies, and stories—helps you know that your child may have a learning difference, *and* your child also has talents and gifts too. Everyone is different. Everyone is unique. Your child with a learning difference is smart—smart in his own way!

By building confidence and joy, and experiencing success, your child can succeed!

Reflections

1. Have you been a parent detective and identified the special talent(s) your child with learning differences possesses?

2. What have you done, or do, to cheer on your child to pursue his or her talent?

3. What else can you do to really be your child's cheerleader?

4. How do you show that you value your child's uniqueness?

5. How much of your time are you willing to contribute to your child's success?

About
Dr. Deborah Ross-Swain, Ed.D., CCC-SLP

Dr. Deborah Ross-Swain is the clinical director and CEO of the Swain Center for Listening, Communicating and Learning and is a certified and licensed speech-language pathologist by the American Speech-Language-Hearing Association (ASHA) and the state of California. Dr. Swain is a former Chief of Speech Pathology at the University of California, Davis Medical Center and held a clinical staff appointment to the School of Medicine. Dr. Swain is the immediate past-president of the California Speech-Language and Hearing Association (CSHA) and served on the CSHA Board of Directors for ten years. Dr. Swain has received the honor of Fellow of the Association as well as awards for Outstanding Service and Outstanding Achievement. Dr. Swain was awarded Outstanding Alumnus in 2016 from California State University, Sacramento. Dr. Swain served on the CSHA Legislative Council and Advisory Council. She currently serves on ASHA's Government Relations and Public Policy Board as well as serving as the chair of CSHA's Early Intervention Committee and the International Committee. Dr. Swain is the author of numerous standardized tests, books, and treatment manuals.

About the Work of Dr. Swain

Dr. Swain is a practicing clinician in the field of speech-language pathology with expertise and passion in the areas of auditory processing, literacy, and learning, as well as early intervention. Dr. Swain is the Clinical Director and CEO of The Swain Center located in Santa Rosa, California, and has been serving her community since 1985. Dr. Swain has a dynamic and dedicated team of professionals working with her to provide an array of services that include Tiny Talkers™, TARPSing™, Let's Adapt™, and JAGuAR™ groups for early intervention, parent education and training, social skills development, and the development of joint attention skills. Dr. Swain consults with parents, professionals, and educators to develop understanding of a child's communication and learning differences in order to develop strategies and interventions to maximize a child's potential for success. Dr. Swain practices and promotes interprofessional practice and education in order to promote success, confidence, and joy in all of the children and their families that are served by her and her clinical team at The Swain Center. Dr. Swain is committed to building confidence and joy in children with learning differences, and gets up each day to give another family hope and another child a dose of confidence and joy! Dr. Swain serves on numerous community and professional associations and organizations. In addition, she is a nationally recognized author, speaker, and researcher, and is a mom of four grown children and Mimi to three grandsons. Dr. Swain would love to hear from you and can be reached at:

dswain@theswaincenter.com or (707) 575-1468

Other Tests and Books by Dr. Ross-Swain

- The Receptive-Expressive Social Communication Assessment-Elementary
- Auditory Processing Disorders: Assessment, Management, and Treatment
- The Listening Inventory
- The Auditory Processing Abilities Test
- The Auditory Phoneme Sequencing Test
- The Ross Information Processing Assessment-2
- A Cognitive-Linguistic Treatment Hierarchy
- The Ross Information Processing Assessment-Geriatric
- The Ross Information Processing Assessment-Pediatric
- The Swallowing Function and Abilities Test
- The Beside Evaluation and Screening Test for Aphasia
- Aphasia Rehabilitation: An Auditory and Verbal Treatment Hierarchy
- Aphasia Rehabilitation: A Reading and Writing Treatment Hierarchy

Connect with
Dr. Deborah Ross-Swain

Address: Deborah Ross-Swain, Ed.D., CCC-SLP
The Swain Center
795 Farmers Lane, Suite 23
Santa Rosa, CA 95405
(707) 575-1468

Website(s): dswain@theswaincenter.com
www.theswaincenter.com
www.confidencejoy.com

Social Media:
Twitter: @swimmerdeb
Facebook: https://m.facebook.com/theswaincenter
LinkedIn: https://www.linkedin.com/in/deb-swain-55705511
Pinterest: www.pinterest.com/theswaincenter.com
Instagram: http://www.instagram.com/the.swain.center

Swain Center:
Facebook: https://m.facebook.com/theswaincenter

About
Dr. Elaine Fogel Schneider, Ph.D., CCC-SLP, BC-DMT, CTTIT

Dr. Elaine Fogel Schneider is the author of the Amazon #1 bestselling book entitled *7 Strategies for Raising Calm, Inspired, & Successful Children.* She is the Executive Director of TouchTime® International. She is a certified and licensed speech-language pathologist by the American Speech-Language-Hearing Association (ASHA) and the state of California, a Board-Certified Dance/Movement Therapist by the American Dance Therapy Association, and a Certified TouchTime® Instructor and Trainer.

Dr. Fogel Schneider is the Vice-President of Professional Services for the California Speech-Language and Hearing Association (CSHA), and has received the honor of Fellow of the Association, as well as awards for Outstanding Service and Caring Communicator. Dr. Fogel Schneider has also been recognized as a Champion of Children by First5 LA, and was awarded the prestigious Jynny Retsinger award from the North Los Angeles County Regional Center for making a difference in the lives of people with disabilities. Dr. Fogel Schneider has also been honored by California's Interagency Coordinating Council for Infants and Toddlers with Disabilities and their Families as the longest-sitting Governor appointee, representing service providers.

She is also the liaison between the Centers for Disease Control's Learn the Signs, Act Early State of California's Advisory Board, and the California Speech Language and Hearing Association.

About the Work of
Dr. Fogel Schneider

Dr. Fogel Schneider "wears many hats" as a practicing clinician in the fields of speech-language pathology, integrated alternative health, and dance-movement therapy, working in private practice, school-based services, and at the University. Her expertise is in areas of interdisciplinary assessments, social-emotional learning, mind-body-spirit integration, communication disorders, infant bonding and attachment, early intervention, and speech sound production and counseling.

She is the creator of BeREALNow® (Be Ready Everyone and Learn Now), a curriculum using the 7 strategies presented in her best-selling book, *7 Strategies for Raising Calm, Inspired & Successful Children,* promoting social-emotional well-being and success. She is committed to each child reaching his or her full potential, confidently and joyfully, with parents being strong advocates for their children.

Dr. Fogel Schneider is a practicing therapist, and serves as a resource and coach to parents who have children with learning differences and special needs. She provides face to face therapy and telehealth for parents, professionals, and children. She is a faculty member at California State University, Los Angeles, a consultant to Long Beach Unified School District's preschool assessment interdisciplinary assessment team, and early childhood programs. As a trainer, coach, and therapist, she enjoys being a resource for physicians, families, and teachers offering strategies for building confidence and joy for children with differences and strengthening families. She is an invited speaker and trainer for school districts, universities, and agencies in the United States and around the world, helping infants and young children with bonding and attachment issues, and children with developmental disabilities and differences.

She speaks with teachers and university students on topics about self-care, reducing burn-out, and many other strategies for their own well-being.

Dr. Fogel Schneider is a world renowned trainer of doctors, nurses, university professors, educators in early childhood education, therapists, home visitors, and special educators for her TouchTime® strategies for bonding and secure attachment with infants and those who care for them. She is also a trainer and keynote speaker for profit and nonprofit organizations, school districts, early childhood programs, special education learning program administrators, foster care agencies, and home visitation programs about using *7 Strategies for Raising Calm, Inspired & Successful Children,* including the *BeREALNow®* program in private schools, community schools, daycare centers, religious schools for children with or without special needs, and in the home.

Dr. Fogel Schneider has utilized the *BeREALNow®* program in preschools with children with special needs, regular kindergarten classrooms, and homes. She is delighted to help others learn these simple strategies to reach their goals, inspiring teachers and providing training on ways to enrich their classrooms and assist children with self-regulation and social-emotional learning. In only five minutes a day, remarkable transformations take place.

Dr. Fogel Schneider has written for popular magazines and professional journals, i.e., *Parents Magazine, Massage Magazine, Tampa Times, Homeschool Handbook, Infants and Young Children, Young Exceptional Child, Zero to Three, American Speech-Language and Hearing Association Perspectives, California Speech-Language-Hearing Magazine,* and more. She is featured on blogs and websites, i.e., parents.com, first5la.

org, breezymama.com, nydailynews.com, Rasmussen.com, webtalkradio.com, brighthubeducation.com, and more.

She appears on national and local television (i.e., being featured on *The Learning Channel* (TLC) and *Fox LA*) and hundreds of radio shows and webinars around the world. As an invited guest by the Vietnamese government, she provided assessments for children with communication and feeding disorders, training in *TouchTime® Communication*, and shared her book *Massaging Your Baby: The* Joy *of TouchTime® Effective Techniques for Happier, Healthier, & Relaxed Child & Parent* with Vietnamese families, university professors, students, and teachers of children with special needs. *Massaging Your Baby – The Joy of TouchTime®,* a valuable resource, has also been translated into Chinese and Malay.

Dr. Fogel Schneider lives in Long Beach, CA with her husband, has one grown daughter, and is "GeeGee" to her two grandchildren. Dr. Fogel Schneider would love to hear from you and can be reached at 1 (888) 871-8803 or via email at drelaine@ askdrelaine.com.

Other Books and Apps by Dr. Fogel Schneider

Amazon #1 Best Seller – *7 Strategies for Raising Calm, Inspired & Successful Children*. Crescendo Publishers, 2016.

Baby Massage Basics. Application for iPhones and iPads, 2014.

Expressions from the Heart Book of Poetry II. 2012.

Expressions from the Heart Book of Poetry I. 2008.

Massaging Your Baby – Effective Techniques for Healthier, Happier, More Relaxed Child & Parent. Square One Publishers, 2006.

Pictures Please – Adult Language Supplement. With Marcia Abbate – co-author. Harper and Row, 2004.

Connect with
Dr. Elaine Fogel Schneider

Address: Elaine Fogel Schneider, Ph.D., CCC-SLP, BC-DMT, CTTIT
TouchTime® International
850 E. Ocean Blvd. Suite 1206
Long Beach, CA 90802

Phone: 1-888-871-8803

Website(s): drelaine@askdrelaine.com
www.askdrelaine.com
www.confidencejoy.com

Social Media:

Facebook: https://www.facebook.com/askdrelaine
https://www.facebook.com/elaine.f.schneider.9
LinkedIn: https://www.linkedin.com/in/dr-elaine-fogel-schneider-3957b42a
Twitter: https://twitter.com/AskDrElaine
Instagram: https://www.instagram/Dr.ElaineFogelSchneider
Pinterest: www.pinterest.com/touchtime

Acknowledgements

The authors want to thank the thousands of clients and their families, professionals, and educators who have served as teachers, mentors, counselors, and colleagues in order to give insight and meaning to this book. We are indebted to our families, who have supported our dreams, visions, efforts, and careers of service. Their unparalleled support and love has given meaning to doing what and why we do what we do.

We thank Robbin Simons and Shayna Rohrig at Crescendo Publishing for their guidance, counsel, and input in the development and publication of this project.

References

Hoque, F. "The 7 Fundamentals of Sustainable Business Growth." *Fast Company.* August 18, 2015. https://www.fastcompany.com/3049856/the-7-fundamentals-of-sustainable-business

Lama, D, and Tutu, D. *The Book of Joy.* New York: Penguin-Random House, 2016.

Learning Disabilities Association of New York State. http://www.ldanys.org/index.php?s=2&b=25

"Learn the Signs: Act Early." *Centers for Disease Control and Prevention.* 2018. http://www.cdc.ncibddd.learnthesignsactearly.gov

Rogers, F. *The World According to Mister Rogers: Important Things to Remember.* New York: Hyperion Books, 2003.

Schneider, Elaine Fogel. "The 6 E's for Maintaining the Innate Passion for Learning." *The Homeschool Handbook* (2017): 14-17.

Schneider, Elaine Fogel. *7 Strategies for Raising Calm, Inspired & Successful Children.* San Diego: Crescendo Press, 2016.

"Team." *Merriam-Webster.* Merriam-Webster, 2011.

Resources

We offer the following as resources for parents, professionals, and educators as potential opportunities to continue learning about ways to build confidence and joy in children with learning differences.

Following are several website resources, listed alphabetically, that are some of our favorites and may be of interest to you:

- www.asha.org
- www.ablekidsfoundation.org
- www.aboutlearningpress.com
- www.adhdchildhood.com
- www.auditoryprocessing.com
- https://childmind.org
- www.csha.org
- http:/drdonnageffner.com
- www.dyslexicadvantage.org
- https//dyslexiaida.org
- www.dyslexia.yale.edu
- http:/edaud.org
- www.ldonline.org
- http://learningaabledkids.com
- www.learningdisability.com
- http://sensoryprocessing101.com
- www.scilearn.com
- www.smartkidswithld.org
- www.specialneeds.com
- http//summitcenter.us

Made in the USA
Monee, IL
16 February 2022

91338425R00095